Isn't It Time For You To Get Over It?

RICK RENNER

A book company anointed to take God's Word
to you and to the nations of the world.

Unless otherwise indicated, all Scripture quotations are taken from the *King James Version* of the Bible.

Isn't It Time for You To Get Over It?
ISBN 0-9725454-1-7
Copyright © 2002 by Rick Renner
P. O. Box 1709
Tulsa, OK 74101-1709

Editorial Consultant: Cynthia Hansen
Cover Design: Randall Miller Design, Inc.
　　　　　　　www.rmdtulsa.com

Printed in the United States of America.
All rights reserved under International Copyright Law. Contents and/or cover may not be reproduced in whole or in part in any form without the express written consent of the Publisher.

Dedication

*I dedicate this book to my mother,
Erlita Renner,
who taught me to walk in love
and to demonstrate the love of Jesus Christ
by serving others.*

*Mother, I want to thank you
for giving your life to serve and assist
so many people
throughout the years.
I cannot imagine a better example than you
of someone who serves others selflessly.
You have been a godly example
to Denise, my boys, and me.*

I love you.

CONTENTS

Chapter One
Everyone Has Opportunities To Get Offended, Upset, Or Really 'Ticked Off' at Someone 9
- You Can Beat Any Temptation! 10
- The Devil Is a Mind Manipulator 12
- There Is a Way Out! 15
- God Will Provide an Escape for You —
  If You Really Want To Be Free 17
- It's Your Choice 18

Chapter Two
Jesus Understands Your Emotions, Frustrations, and Temptations 21
- Jesus Is Touched With the Feeling
  Of Your Infirmities 23
- Jesus Was Tempted
  To Get Offended and Upset 26
- People's Behavior Can Be Surprising,
  Shocking, and Inconsistent 28
- Is This an Opportunity for the Holy Spirit
  To Deal With *You*? 33
- A True-Life Example 37
- Jesus Understands and Wants
  To Set You Free 40

Chapter Three
**How the Devil Operates
In the Realm of the Mind and Emotions** ...43
   Standing Against the Wiles of the Devil 44
   What Are the 'Wiles' of the Devil? 46
   The Devil's Destination and Desire 48
   Mark 11:23 Works for the Devil Too 51
   Out of the Abundance of the Heart 53
   An Emotional Puppet
      Or a Renewed Mind? 55
   Someone Is Going To Control Your Mind,
      So Who Is It Going To Be? 57
   What Does the Name 'Devil' Mean? 60
   Don't Give the Devil a Chance To Get
      In the Middle of Your Relationships 63
   A Relationship-Breaker
      From the Beginning of Time 66
   Are Your Relationships a Joy or a Curse? ...67

Chapter Four
**Judas Iscariot — The Friend
Who Became Jesus' Betrayer** 69
   How Did One of Jesus' Disciples
      Become His Betrayer? 70
   Mary's Lavishly Expensive Gift 71
   Mary's Expression of Appreciation
      For Jesus 73
   An Opportunity for Bitterness,
      Resentment, and Offense 76

    Jesus' Words Could Have Offended
       Anyone Listening 77
    How Did the Devil Get a Foothold
       In the Mind and Heart of Judas? 78
    When Satan Tried To Use Me
       As a Betrayer 85
    Questions To Ask When Something
       Is Becoming a Major Issue to You 88
    It's Time To Make an Examination
       Of Your Heart 89

Chapter Five

You Are the Bishop of Your Own Heart 91
    Keep the Weeds Out of Your Own 'Garden' . .95
    God Holds Us All Responsible 98
    Stay Out of the Judgment Business 103
    Let God's Grace Help You! 105
    You Have No Excuses To Stay
       The Way You Are 109
    How's Your Memory Working? 111

Chapter Six

What Is a 'Root of Bitterness'? 117
    Tell-Tale Signs That Bitterness
       Is Growing in Your Life 119
    Be Careful What You Dump on People
       Who Are Listening to You! 123
    You *Will* Have an Opportunity
       To Get Offended! 127
    What if *You* Are the Offended One? 131

Chapter Seven
It's Time for You To Let It Go! 133
- How To Confront Someone 136
- What Does the Word 'Forgive'
  Really Mean? 142
- It's Time To Let It Go! 142
- Taking It to the Next Level 144

Chapter Eight
**Why Jesus Compared Unforgiveness
To the Sycamine Tree** 149
- Important Facts About the Sycamine Tree .. 150
- It's Time To *Uproot* and *Remove* That Tree! 158
- Command Those Attitudes
  To Be Planted in the Sea! 161

Chapter Nine
**Ten Practical Suggestions
To Keep Your Heart Free
Of Bitterness, Unforgiveness, and Strife** .. 165
- Suggestion #1 166
- Suggestion #2 171
- Suggestion #3 173
- Suggestion #4 176
- Suggestion #5 178
- Suggestion #6 180
- Suggestion #7 183
- Suggestion #8 185
- Suggestion #9 187
- Suggestion #10 188
- So What Are You Going To Do? 190

CHAPTER ONE

Everyone Has Opportunities To Get Offended, Upset, Or Really 'Ticked Off' at Someone

The fact that you've picked up this book tells me you are seeking answers about how to deal with *bitterness, resentment,* and *unforgiveness.*

Everyone has had to deal with these issues at one time or another. So as we get started, I want you to know first of all that you are not alone in your struggles to combat this internal problem of bitterness and resentment. You also don't need to feel embarrassed about your dilemma because it's something everyone faces at some point. But at the same time, don't accept unforgiveness as an inevitable part of your life. With the help found in this book, you can walk free of these negative attitudes that have kept you bound.

So I urge you to stay with me all the way to the end of this book. I intend to take you on a path that will show you how to permanently *uproot* and *remove* bitterness, resentment, and unforgiveness from your life!

You Can Beat Any Temptation!

All temptations can be beaten! You just have to make up your mind that you're going to be the *conqueror* and not the *conquered*! This is certainly true when it comes to conquering the temptation to get upset or resentful toward someone.

You may not have thought of it before, but getting hurt and offended is a *temptation*. It's a moment when something happens or a thought goes through your mind that induces you to get upset or to become angry.

Everyone Has Opportunities To Get Offended, Upset, Or Really 'Ticked Off' at Someone

Those thoughts and emotions act as a stimulant to get you all stirred up. Nevertheless, in that moment you are consciously aware that you can let the temptation to be offended pass you by, or you can allow the thoughts to fester in your mind and emotions until the offense becomes a major issue. ==It's a choice you make.==

It's similar to a sexual temptation. You can choose to turn and look the other way, or you can dwell on that temptation until it fills your mind and imagination. Likewise, if you choose to meditate on the perceived offense, it won't be too long until the devil convinces you that you've been wronged or treated unjustly and that you have every right to nurse that grudge.

If you don't put on the brakes with those thoughts, your relationship with that person or group of people will soon be negatively affected by hurt feelings, offense, and grievances. This is certain to happen, whether the offense is real or imagined.

You see, it may be hard to believe, but most grievances are more imagined than real. Most offenses are a result of misunderstanding and miscommunication blown clear out of proportion rather than of direct attacks from others. Just as the three little pigs had to deal with the "big bad wolf" in the popular fairy tale, we also have an enemy who is waiting to huff and puff and blow away our peace and joy in relationships!

The Devil Is a Mind Manipulator

The devil is a master when it comes to mind manipulation. He knows that if he can get you to spend a little time meditating on a wrong that was done to you, the perceived wrong will get blown out of proportion until you finally become ensnared in *bitterness, resentment,* and *unforgiveness.*

Never forget that Satan was kicked out of Heaven because of his ability to create confusion and discord! Heaven is as perfect as an environment can be. Yet in that perfect environment, the devil was able to affect one-third of the angels with his smooth but totally slanderous allegations against God.

Angels who had worshipped together for eons of time now stood *opposed* to each other over nonexistent issues the devil had conjured up in their minds. In fact, Satan was so adept at distorting truth that he was able to lure one-third of them into rebelling against Almighty God!

If the devil is persuasive enough to deceive brilliant, mighty, powerful angels, how much more easily can he deceive people — *who live in a far-from-perfect environment and wrestle daily with their own imperfections, as well as with the imperfections of others.* The emotional makeup of human beings makes them even more susceptible to the devil's masterful skills of lying, deception, and manipulation.

Satan watches for the right timing. He comes along at an opportune moment. He waits until you're *tired, weary,* or *exasperated.* Perhaps you woke up in a bad mood; someone gave you a "look" you didn't like; or you just started your day off on the wrong foot. Then suddenly someone does something totally unexpected that you don't like — *something that takes you off guard and by surprise*!

At first, you're *shocked*. Then you start to feel *hurt*. As the day passes and you keep thinking about what happened, the *hurt* turns into *anger*! Before you know it, that event is so exaggerated in your mind, you can no longer see it in its true perspective.

That's when the devil whispers: *You have been so mistreated. If anyone has a reason to be offended, it's you! No one appreciates you! All you do is give, give, and give. What do you get in return? Nothing! You ought to back out of everything you're doing and just let people sit in their own mess!*

Poor ol' you! After all you've done to show your love and to sacrifice for others, what have others done for you? You ought to just walk out on all these ingrates you've been serving and trying to help. They don't appreciate you anyway!

It's totally understandable that your feelings are hurt! Hang on to those grudges, and don't ever let anyone hurt you like this again!

When thoughts like these deluge your mind, you need to know that it is Satan setting a trap in front of you. He is trying to ensnare you so he can cripple you emotionally and cut you off from the people you love. He's trying to get you to bite the bait so *he can set the hook*!

There Is a Way Out!

You don't have to fall into this trap anymore! If you really want out of this type of emotional quandary, there is a way out.

First Corinthians 10:13 promises, "There hath no temptation taken you but such as is common to man: but God is faithful, who will not suffer you to be tempted above that ye are able; but will with the temptation also make a way to escape, that ye may be able to bear it."

This verse says that God will make a way for you to escape any temptation that comes against you. This even includes those moments when you are tempted to get upset with someone or to allow your feelings to get hurt.

According to First Corinthians 10:13, God will make a way for you to escape — *if* you really want to escape!

- *You don't have to give in to the temptation to get your feelings hurt all the time.*

- *You don't have to walk around "wearing your feelings on your shoulder" anymore.*

- *You don't have to feel crushed and hurt when others fail your expectations of them.*

- *You don't have to continue living in this prison of bitterness, resentment, and unforgiveness.*

God Will Provide an Escape for You — *If* You Really Want To Be Free

God will make a way for you to escape these negative emotions, *if* you really want to escape them. But you are the only one who can make the choice to jump through that escape hatch!

Millions of Christians are held captive by bitterness, resentment, and unforgiveness because they will *not* take the leap through that escape hatch. As a result, they have no joy, no peace, and no victory in their lives. They may be Christians, but they're miserable because they haven't made the choice to jump through the escape hatch God has provided for them and leave all that negative garbage behind.

If you'll say yes to the Lord, He will show you how to get out of this mess! You can *avoid, evade, dodge, elude, shake off, get out of,* and *break away from* every temptation to take offense. You never have to get dragged into destructive emotions, feelings, and attitudes.

It's Your Choice

There are millions of unhappy Christians who are inwardly miserable because they keep pushing the rewind button in their minds. They keep going back and replaying every grievance ever done to them. *They have replayed these offenses again and again and again.*

You are *the only one* who can choose to walk out of these killer attitudes. The moment you make that decision, your journey to freedom has begun!

So today the Lord is asking you:

"Are you going to stay the way you are right now, or are you willing to take the proper steps to escape from this emotional temptation and demonic trap?

"Are you ready to give up all unforgiveness, laying it at the foot of the Cross so you can walk free? Or do you want to continue clinging to that resentment and turmoil, held hostage by those

spiritually, mentally, and physically crippling attitudes?"

What is your answer? What are you going to do? God is waiting for you to decide if you will receive the freedom He is offering you or remain a hostage for the rest of your life. *The choice is yours to make.*

In this book, I want to show you how to get from where you are to the place of liberty Jesus Christ purchased for you!

CHAPTER TWO

Jesus Understands Your Emotions, Frustrations, And Temptations

If you've ever been in this situation I'm talking about — controlled by hurt feelings and offenses — you know it is a miserable state to be in.

Everyone has opportunities to get offended, upset, or "ticked off" at someone. So when someone does something disappointing to you, how successful are you at dealing with it? *Be honest!*

- *Are you dealing with hurt feelings or offense toward anyone in your life right now?*

Isn't It Time for You To Get Over It?

- *Is there one particular person who easily throws you into an emotional tizzy that tears you up on the inside?*

- *Do you find that the devil uses one person or one particular situation over and over to steal your peace and joy?*

- *Is there a person in your life whom you love but whose insensitivity to your feelings frequently shocks and hurts you?*

- *Do you harbor ill feelings toward someone? Do you wish you didn't feel the way you do about him or her?*

- *Are you emotionally paralyzed by what that person did or failed to do?*

- *Are you free from offense, or are you a prisoner of hurt feelings?*

- *Do you allow offense to roll around in your head and emotions until it finally begins to "tick you off"?*

- *Have you tried unsuccessfully to conquer bitterness in prayer? Have you so far been unable to fully forgive the person and release the offense?*

We've all been offended from time to time by something someone said or did or by what he or she *didn't* say or do. Sometimes we are even tempted to get easily offended by a "look" someone gives us. Offense is something *everyone* has to deal with at one time or another.

Jesus Is Touched With the Feelings of Your Infirmities

Jesus Christ empathizes with every temptation and struggle you face in this life. He *identifies* and *sympathizes* with you. He has *compassion* for you in regard to what you're feeling and the situation you're facing.

Hebrews 4:15 says, "For we have not an high priest which cannot be touched with the feeling of our infirmities; but was in all points tempted like as we are, yet without sin." This verse declares that when Jesus walked on the earth, He was God in the flesh; yet He faced *every* temptation you and I face in life.

This is one reason Jesus understands the emotions, frustrations, and temptations you face in life. He has been where you are. He has felt what you feel. He has overcome the temptations you are now trying to overcome.

Hebrews 4:15 says we have a priest who is "...touched with the feelings of our infirmities...." This is why the next verse urges us, "Let us therefore come boldly unto the throne of grace, that we may obtain mercy, and find grace to help in time of need" (v. 16).

If Jesus was really tempted in all points as you are, this means:

- *If you're tempted to steal, Jesus was tempted to steal too.*

- *If you're tempted to lie, Jesus was also tempted to lie.*

**Jesus Understands
Your Emotions, Frustrations,
And Temptations**

- *If you're tempted sexually, Jesus was confronted by sexual temptation too.*

- *If you're tempted to wear your feelings on your shoulder and get your feelings hurt all the time, Jesus was tempted to feel this way as well.*

- *If you're tempted to hate and to hold a grudge, Jesus was tempted to hate and to be a grudge-holder too.* (Just think how you might be tempted to feel if Judas had betrayed you!)

- *If you're tempted to be offended, Jesus was also tempted to be offended.*

- *If you're tempted to give up and quit, Jesus was tempted to give up and quit too.*

There is no need to feel too embarrassed to go to Jesus! If anyone can understand what you are going through right now, *it is Jesus*! He has been tempted in all points just like you, yet He never succumbed to temptation. Because of what Jesus went through:

- *He understands your dilemma.*

- *He has experienced your problem.*

- *He is familiar with disappointment.*

- *He knows the temptation to get frustrated.*

- *He sympathizes when you get upset.*

That's why Hebrews 4:16 says to come *boldly* to the throne of grace!

As One who has faced every temptation you personally face, Jesus is on your side and is standing by to help. Hebrews 4:16 promises that when you come to Him for help, you can obtain mercy and find grace to help in time of need.

Jesus Was Tempted To Get Offended and Upset

You may ask, "Rick, how do you know that Jesus was tempted to get offended and upset or to allow His feelings to get hurt?"

**Jesus Understands
Your Emotions, Frustrations,
And Temptations**

The Bible very clearly states that Jesus faced *each temptation* you and I face in life. Jesus never fell into one of Satan's traps, but He definitely faced these frustrations. You see, if Jesus hadn't been tempted by every temptation as we are, He wouldn't be able to understand us and serve as our great High Priest.

I can only imagine the frustration Jesus must have felt in the Garden of Gethsemane. He had invested three and a half years of His life into His disciples. Now for the first time, Jesus needed *them.*

Jesus asked three of His disciples to pray for Him during His hour of temptation (Matthew 26:37-45). He only asked them for one hour of prayer, but instead of praying, they fell asleep. He came and pleaded with them a second time to pray with Him, but once more they fell asleep. For a third time, Jesus came and besought His disciples to pray, but again they fell asleep on the job.

What if you had been in Jesus' shoes that night? What if you had given three years of your life to these disciples — but when you asked them to help you for the first time, *they kept failing you again and again?*

It would be normal for a person in this situation to be tempted to become resentful, upset, or even offended. Anyone in that position would be tempted to think, *How dare you sleep on the job after all I've done for you! I'm sorry I ever did anything for you bunch of ingrates!*

Jesus never fell into the trap of *bitterness, resentment,* or *unforgiveness.* As He hung on the Cross, He prayed, "...Father, forgive them..." (Luke 23:34).

People's Behavior Can Be Surprising, Shocking, and Inconsistent

Do your best to understand people, but never be too shocked if people do something that surprises you!

**Jesus Understands
Your Emotions, Frustrations,
And Temptations**

People can be quite a mystery! You finally think you have them all figured out, and then they do something else that totally blows your mind! You never would have dreamed in a million years that they'd do something so crazy or inconsistent! That's why if you're going to live a happy life, you have to learn how to *forgive and overlook* people's inconsistencies, lack of commitment, unfaithfulness, temper tantrums, and mood swings — as well as all the other defects connected with being a human being.

There are days when I don't even understand my own moods! Therefore, I know I have to show mercy when I see others act differently than I expected them to do. When I'm tempted to get upset with Denise, my kids, or my associates in the ministry, I stop and remind myself that I'm not perfect either. I'm sure there are moments when these same people are just as bewildered by me as I am by them!

- *Do you always understand your own moods?*

Isn't It Time for You To Get Over It?

- *Do you always have a grip on your own emotions?*

- *Do you ever do anything that's inconsistent with what you know is right?*

- *Do you ever fall short of the standards you set and demand of those around you?*

I can't complain too much about others being a mystery because I'm such a mystery to myself sometimes! Oh, how I long for the day when I walk in the Spirit 100% of the time! Unfortunately, it looks like that won't happen until my mortal flesh puts on incorruption!

When we receive our glorified bodies and go to Heaven, all our inconsistencies, mood swings, double standards, and complex emotions will be gone. *We'll be in good moods forever!* Until then, we have to stay in an attitude of forgiveness and extend the same mercy to others that we expect them to extend to us.

**Jesus Understands
Your Emotions, Frustrations,
And Temptations**

Forgive me for being so gut-level honest, but until that day when the entire Body of Christ sees Jesus face to face, believers will experience moments when:

- *Husbands' behavior shocks their wives.*

- *Wives make their husbands mad.*

- *Children disappoint their parents.*

- *Parents lose their tempers with their kids and hurt their children's feelings.*

- *Friends are nowhere to be found when they are desperately needed.*

- *Employees stab their fellow employees in the back to get a better job or promotion.*

- *Employers play favorites with employees rather than dealing fairly and justly as they should.*

- *Church members betray their pastor by talking behind his back.*

Isn't It Time for You To Get Over It?

- *Pastors occasionally repeat what was told to them in confidence, wounding and hurting the church member who privately confided in him.*

Even Christians who spend hours in prayer, read the Word, pray in the Spirit, and seek to live a holy life sometimes get in the flesh, doing and saying things they later regret. *It's just part of being human.*

If you're going to get "bent out of shape" and upset every time someone says or does something *below* what you expect of them, you will live your life constantly bothered, upset, and frustrated. Similarly, if you're going to lose your peace every time someone *doesn't* do what you expect of them, you're going to live a roller-coaster existence — *up and down, up and down.*

**Jesus Understands
Your Emotions, Frustrations,
And Temptations**

Is This an Opportunity For the Holy Spirit To Deal With *You*?

Rather than focus on the inconsistencies, flukes, and flaws of others, why not look in the mirror and let the Holy Spirit deal with *you* about the areas *you* need to change? It may be that God is using the people you think have done you so wrong to *expose* something in your own character that needs to change!

That's why it's so important to always ask yourself, *Has this situation revealed that:*

- *I lack patience?*

- *I lack longsuffering?*

- *I lack kindness?*

- *I lack temperance?*

- *I am unforgiving?*

- *I am a grudge-holder?*

Isn't It Time for You To Get Over It?

- *I am intolerant?*

- *I am a complainer?*

- *I am judgmental?*

- *I am critical?*

- *I am unsympathetic?*

- *I am fault-finding?*

God wants to change you too. If this relationship or situation has revealed a weakness in your own character, it's time to stop looking at the faults of others and let God's Spirit teach you to overcome your own exposed faults.

Galatians 5:22,23 says, "But the fruit of the Spirit is love, joy, peace, longsuffering, gentleness, goodness, faith, meekness, temperance: against such there is no law." A mature Christian must learn to let the fruit of the Spirit operate in him or her regardless of the situation.

Jesus Understands Your Emotions, Frustrations, And Temptations

When your relationships with others are going great — when you have no challenges, no problems, and no conflicts with anyone — it's easy to be kind, loving, longsuffering, and easy to get along with. The real proof of spiritual maturity isn't measured by the moments when your flesh is comfortable. *Your real spirituality is revealed when you run into a situation that rubs your flesh the wrong way!* In those moments:

- *Are you able to crucify your flesh?*

- *Are you able to esteem others above yourself?*

- *Are you able to think of the interests and concerns of others?*

In order to live a happy Christian life, you *must* develop the fruit of the Spirit in your spiritual walk. If you try to base your joy and happiness on other people, you'll *never* be happy. You'll end up feeling let down, hurt, disappointed, wounded, and angry. Other people will never be able to do enough to make you happy all the time.

On the other hand, when you develop the fruit of the Spirit in your life, you can be happy in any environment because your happiness will come from within; it won't be affected by people or by outside circumstances.

Some have tried to find their meaning and fulfillment in other people for so long and have been let down so many times that they have become bitter and resentful. If this situation persists over a long period of time, these bad attitudes will begin to color their entire perspective of life and make them completely miserable — even if they call themselves "Spirit-filled Christians."

If you have harbored these types of unhealthy attitudes, you must allow them to be *recognized, uprooted* and *removed* by the Spirit of God. Otherwise, they will begin to produce vile fruit that has the power to *socially isolate* you and *emotionally immobilize* you for the rest of your life.

Left untended, *bitterness, resentment,* and *unforgiveness* become like a terminal disease. These deadly attitudes eventually begin to eat away at your insides, turning you bitter and destroying every relationship in your life.

A True-Life Example

Let me tell you of a true-life example that illustrates the destructive effects of bitterness, resentment, unforgiveness, and offense.

I'm thinking of a precious woman in Riga, Latvia, whom I have known for years. She is one of these emotional prisoners about whom I am writing. She may be free to walk the streets of Riga, but she is just as bound as any person I've ever ministered to in a real prison.

There are *reasons* why this woman is bitter and resentful. Her early life was filled with hurt and abuse. But she has never been able to forgive those who hurt her and, as a result, has been captive for many years.

She was just one of millions who were mistreated during the Soviet years. Many people could tell a similar story, but they have learned to forgive, forget, and move on. This woman has never been able to let the past be buried. Captivated by these hurts, she now lives in a very lonely and solitary world. Week after week, she sits alone in the balcony of the church, not allowing anyone to touch her, talk to her, or get close to her in any way.

Resentment and *unforgiveness* has caused her to *prejudge* everyone who tries to draw near to her. Her past wounds have become an excuse for not trusting people and for accusing the entire Body of Christ of being hypocrites. But what she accuses others of is *exactly* what she has become.

Her whole appearance and speech has become stern and harsh. Her body is filled with a crippling, debilitating arthritis. She is the *exact reflection* of the hatred she carries in her soul.

This may sound like an extreme case; I wish it were. But, sadly, it is a very real scenario for many believers. The truth is, the Body of Christ is loaded with people who carry scars from the past that affect their present lives and relationships.

If you've ever been abused, hurt, let down, wounded, deserted, or betrayed by your spouse; stabbed in the back by fellow church members; or rejected by your parents, family or friends; then you know how the devil can use such an event to debilitate you. But it's time to move on and let the past be the past.

If you carry wounds, bruises, and scars from previous hurts and offenses, you don't have to carry them anymore. *You don't have to live with the residual effect of what the devil did to you in the past.*

Jesus Understands and Wants To Set You Free

At the beginning of this chapter, I wrote that everyone has an opportunity to get upset or offended. The devil will make sure that opportunity comes your way! It is important that you know how to respond to these opportunities so you don't get entangled in the devil's snares.

In the next chapter, I want to explain to you *exactly* how the devil operates in the realm of your emotions. If you understand the tactics he uses, you can thwart his attacks before he sows bad seed into your soul. This next chapter may be the life-saving revelation you've been crying out for God to send you!

However, let me first encourage you to do this: Before you blame others for their failures or point your finger at the devil, go to the mirror of God's Word and ask yourself:

**Jesus Understands
Your Emotions, Frustrations,
And Temptations**

- *How do I need to change?*

- *How can I become more understanding?*

- *How can I develop more patience in my life?*

- *How can I extend mercy to those who hurt me?*

- *How can I correct weak areas in my character that have been exposed by these circumstances?*

Jesus understands your struggles with bitterness and resentment. He had to overcome the same type of temptations Himself! So the next time you're feeling hurt and offended because of other people's behavior, get quiet in your heart and listen to the voice of His Spirit. Ask Him to reveal to you what needs to change in your own life. That's the first step in walking out of the bondage of bitterness into the freedom of forgiveness!

CHAPTER THREE

How the Devil Operates in the Realm Of the Mind and Emotions

In this chapter, I want to help you understand how the devil works in the realm of the mind and emotions. What I am about to tell you is so simple; yet it is also life-changing and revolutionary. If you grab hold of these truths, it can set you free from the devil's lies forever!

Let me begin by saying that the devil has no right to operate in your life unless you open a door for him to come in and do his business. Therefore, when you keep wrong attitudes out of your life, you make it very difficult for the devil to find an entrance into your family, friendships, relationships, health, finances, ministry, or business.

When the devil can't come in the front door, he often seeks a way to get in through the *back* door. One back door he uses is *bitterness*, *resentment*, and *unforgiveness*. These attitudes create an entrance for Satan to intrude right into the middle of your most vital relationships. And believe me, keeping the devil *out* of your relationships is far easier than trying to *remove* him after he's already found his way inside!

However, if the devil has already gotten a foothold in any area of your life through these destructive attitudes, I'm here to tell you that *you can still walk free!*

Standing Against the Wiles of the Devil

In Ephesians 6:10-18, Paul explicitly tells us how the devil operates. This passage of Scripture is extremely important for you to know and understand. (I recommend that you read my book, *Dressed To Kill*, which deals expressly with the issues of *spiritual warfare and spiritual weaponry*.)

In Ephesians 6:11, Paul writes, "Put on the whole armour of God, that ye may be able to stand against the wiles of the devil." I want you to especially pay attention to the phrase "the wiles of the devil." Understanding the meaning of this phrase will give you insight into the way the devil attempts to operate in a person's life.

However, three other key New Testament words to understand as well are the words "devices," "deception," and "devil." Once you see how these words relate to each another, I believe a veil will be lifted and the light of revelation will shine in your heart, causing you to understand how the devil tries to operate in most people's lives, *including your own*.

Stay with me now as I take you on a Greek word study you will never forget! Pick up your highlighter and get ready to mark up this section of the book, because you will want to refer to it again and again.

What Are the 'Wiles' of the Devil?

The word "wiles" is taken from the word *methodos*. It is a compound of the words *meta* and *odos*. The word *meta* is a preposition that means *with*. The word *odos* is the word for a *road*. When the words *meta* and *odos* are compounded into one word, as in Ephesians 6:11, it literally means *with a road*.

You've probably already figured out that the word *methodos* is where we get the word "method." Some translations actually translate the word *methodos* in Ephesians 6:11 as the word "method," but the word "method" is *not* strong enough to convey the full meaning of the Greek word *methodos* ("wiles").

Let me make the meaning of this word real simple for you. As I said, the most literal meaning of the word "wiles" (*methodos*) is *with a road*.

How the Devil Operates in the Realm Of the Mind and Emotions

I realize this seems strange, but when you connect this to the devil as Paul does in Ephesians 6:11, it means that *the devil travels on one road, one lane, one path, or one avenue.* In other words, *he possesses only one approach to you.*

I realize that many believers think the devil has all kinds of imaginary ways to find access into their lives. However, the word *methodos* tells us that the enemy *doesn't* have a whole bunch of tricks in his bag. He only has *one approach* or *one way* to get into a person's life.

Let me give you an example of what I mean. If you're going to take a trip, the logical thing for you to do is to get a map and chart your journey to your destination. You don't take just any ol' road; rather, you strategize to find the best and fastest way to get where you're going. *Right?*

It would be pretty foolish for you to jump in the car and take off with no sense of direction. Taking any ol' road could lead you in a multitude of wrong directions. It's just better to use a map and stay on track. *Right?*

This is precisely the idea of the word *methodos*. The devil isn't wasting any time. He knows where he wants to go. He has chosen his destination. Rather than mess around on a bunch of different routes, he has mastered the best way to get where he wants to go.

The devil is *not* a mindless traveler. When he arrives at his place of destination, he has one main goal he wants to accomplish: He wants to wreak havoc and bring destruction. That's what the enemy attempts to do whenever and wherever he shows up.

Therefore, we must ask: *"Where is the devil traveling, and what does he want to do once he gets there?"*

The Devil's Destination and Desire

I believe Paul answers the question about Satan's destination in Second Corinthians 2:11 when he says, "…we are not ignorant of his [Satan's] *devices.*"

How the Devil Operates in the Realm Of the Mind and Emotions

Pay careful attention to the word "devices" in this verse. It is the Greek word *noemata*, a form of the word *nous*. *Nous* is the Greek word for the *mind* or the *intellect*. Thus, in one sense Paul is saying, *"...we are not ignorant of Satan's mind"* or *"...we are not ignorant of the way Satan schemes and thinks."*

But the word *noemata* also denotes Satan's insidious plot to fill the human mind with *confusion*. There is no doubt that the mind is the arena where Satan feels most comfortable. He knows if he can access a person's mind and emotions, he will very likely be able to snare and entrap that individual.

One writer says that the word *noemata* not only depicts Satan's scheming mind, but also his crafty, subtle way of attacking and victimizing *others'* minds. Another expositor says that the word "devices" can even carry the notion of *mind games*. This means you could translate the verse, *"...we are not ignorant of Satan's mind games."*

I personally like this translation because I believe it identifies the primary destination of the devil — *to get into a person's mind and fill it with lying emotions, false perceptions, and confusion.* It was for this reason that Paul urged us, "Casting down imaginations, and every high thing that exalteth itself against the knowledge of God, and bringing into captivity every thought to the obedience of Christ" (2 Corinthians 10:5).

The devil loves to make a playground out of people's minds and emotions! He delights in filling their perceptions and senses with illusions that captivate them, paralyze them, and ultimately destroy them — *just like the woman I told you about in the previous chapter.*

Rather than fall victim to the devil's attacks, you must make a mental decision to take charge of your mind and emotions. Take *every* thought captive to the obedience of Christ!

But if you're going to beat the devil at this game, you have to put all your energy into taking every thought captive. And once you make the decision to do it, *you have to stick with it*. If you're not really committed to seizing *every* thought the devil tries to inject into your mind and emotions, he'll strike you again!

For example, the devil may try to tell you, *You're a failure. You're a failure. You're a failure.* These mental assaults will produce nothing as long as you resist them. But the day you begin to believe those lies and perceive them as truth, you're in trouble.

If you don't quickly abort the devil's deceptive thoughts, it won't be long until your faith gives power to that lie and causes it to become a bona fide reality in your life. *You will become a failure!*

Mark 11:23 Works for the Devil Too

Mark 11:23 is a powerful verse about faith and confession that believers claim and use. *But the principle in this verse works for the devil too.* The verse says, "For verily I say unto you, That whosoever shall say unto this mountain, Be thou removed, and be thou cast into the sea; and shall not doubt in his heart, but shall believe that those things which he saith shall come to pass; he shall have whatsoever he saith."

According to what Jesus taught in this verse, you can bring to pass whatsoever you say and *believe in your heart*. For instance, if you believe in your heart that Jesus purchased your healing and you put your *heartfelt faith* together with the *confession of your mouth*, you can literally bring that healing into manifestation in your physical body.

Creative power is released when the heart and mouth get in agreement! That's why you must be careful about what you believe in your heart and say with your mouth, because when your heart and mouth get "in sync," it makes things happen!

This *heart-mouth combination* works on both the positive and the negative side. It can bring about the manifestation of healing to your body, salvation to your family, prosperity to your business, and growth to your church. *But the devil also knows how to use this principle against you!* He knows that if he can fill your mind and heart with lies that you believe and then coax you to start confessing those lies with your mouth, *you will make those evil images come to pass!*

That's why the devil wants to fill your mind with deceptive thoughts. That's why he paints lies so vividly on the "movie screen" in your mind. That's why he assaults your mind and emotions *again, again,* and *again.* Satan knows if he can get you to embrace these evil mental images, you'll start speaking them out of your mouth — *and if you start speaking them, you will bring them into manifestation.*

Out of the Abundance of the Heart

Jesus said, "…out of the abundance of the heart the mouth speaketh" (Matthew 12:34). *According to Jesus, whatever is in your heart is eventually going to come out of your mouth!*

Because great power is released when your heart and mouth start working together, it's extremely important that you put the right things *in* your heart. When you bring your heart and mouth into agreement with God's Word, you are moving into the realm of creative faith.

Mark 11:23 promises that whatever you believe in your heart and say with your mouth *will* come to pass. But as I said before, this doesn't just apply to Bible promises; it applies to *anything* you believe in your heart and say with your mouth. So if the devil can get you to believe and say wrong things, your own heart and mouth will cause those killer confessions to come to pass.

I know it's hard to control your mouth sometimes. But when you start to "run at the mouth" and say any ol' thing the devil puts in your mind, you're playing with *fire*!

It is a scientific fact that when you speak something *out loud*, those words are verified and empowered in your mind. That's why the devil wants you to repeat every stupid thing he puts in your head. By repeating it out loud, you are helping him build a *stronghold* in the realm of your mind.

An Emotional Puppet Or a Renewed Mind?

Once the devil has established a stronghold in your mind, it's just a matter of time until he starts pulling your emotional strings. He wants to make you an *emotional puppet* of his own design!

You see, whoever controls your mind also controls your emotions. And whoever controls your emotions has the supreme power to affect your self-image, your marriage, your friendships, your relationships, the way you project yourself to others, and so on.

This is another reason why it's so important for you to spend time in the Word of God. As you spend time meditating in the Word, your mind is *renewed* to God's way of thinking (Ephesians 4:23;

Colossians 3:10). God's Word brings a supernatural cleansing that washes your mind and emotions from the contamination of the world, the memories of past bad experiences, and the lies the enemy has tried to sow into your brain.

When you make it a priority to fill your mind with truth from God's Word, you make it difficult for the enemy to penetrate your mind. And if he can't penetrate your mind, he can't touch your emotions either. On the other hand, your own failure to fill your mind with God's Word could result in catastrophe as every area of your life is left vulnerable to Satan's assaults.

A person whose mind is renewed to the Word of God is strengthened and undergirded inwardly. He is harder to deceive because his strong foundation of truth repels the enemy's attacks.

Satan knows that empty heads are easy to deceive. That's why he just loves it when he finds a believer who has made no effort to fill his or her mind with truth from God's Word. *The enemy has found another empty head just waiting for someone to come along and fill it — and he's happy to oblige!*

Someone Is Going To Control Your Mind, So Who Is It Going To Be?

Your mind is going to be filled with *something*, so you may as well choose the right thing to fill it. Who or what is going to control your mind? *God and His Word? Or the enemy and his lies?* Your choice in this matter will determine your successes or your failures in life, so make sure you choose wisely.

I want to give you an example of what happens when people let the enemy take control of their minds and emotions. Let's talk about the very basic example of marriage.

Many marriages fail because of lies the devil pounds into the minds of one or both spouses. For example, the devil may whisper to the wife, *Your marriage is in trouble. Your marriage is in trouble.* At first, the wife recognizes this thought as a lie from the enemy. She knows their marriage has never been better! Yet the enemy continues to pound away at her mind — *striking, battering, beating, hammering, and clobbering her* mentally and emotionally with lying allegations:

- *This relationship can't stay this strong forever.*

- *This is too good to be true.*

- *This marriage won't last long.*

- *This dream is about to burst.*

The wife may know these thoughts are preposterous. But if she doesn't *rebuke* and *reject* these doubt-filled thoughts, they will begin to take her to the next level of mental accusations, such as:

- *He can't love you this much.*

- *He is interested in someone else.*

How the Devil Operates in the Realm Of the Mind and Emotions

- *He doesn't send you flowers anymore.*

- *He looks at other women with interest.*

- *There is something wrong.*

- *Your marriage is in serious trouble.*

- *It's time for you to get a lawyer!*

The moment husbands and wives begin to dwell on this kind of devilish propaganda, the door is thrown open for the enemy to really begin pounding their minds relentlessly. At that point, they will live with a torrent of tormenting and harassing thoughts about their marriage until they put their foot down and command the devil to *stop*!

The devil is *extremely proficient* at bombarding people's minds and emotions with his lies and deceptions until they accept those lies as truth. *The truth is, he has walloped the human race through his strategy of mind control!* That's why half the world takes medication for depression and spends loads of money buying self-help books.

As a believer, however, there is never a need for you to be whacked by the devil's intimidations, suggestions, or lies. He may hammer as vigorously and persistently as he can, but the devil is simply not able to penetrate your life when you're safeguarded by *the shield of faith* (Ephesians 6:16) and your mind is fortified by the *helmet of salvation* (Ephesians 6:17).

What Does the Name 'Devil' Mean?

The name "devil" comes from the Greek word *diabalos*. But this Greek word *diabalos* is much more than a name — *it's a job description*! It tells you *how* the devil operates and *what* he wants to try to achieve in your mind, emotions, and, ultimately, in every area of your life, *including your relationships.*

The word *diabolos* is a compound of the words *dia* and *balos*. The word *dia* means *through*, as in

How the Devil Operates in the Realm Of the Mind and Emotions

the sense of *someone piercing something through one side to the other.* Used as a prefix in the name "devil" (*diabalos*), it presents the picture of *Satan's ability to pierce or to penetrate.*

The word *balos* means to *throw*, such as in *throwing a ball or rock*. It describes a *fast-forward, hurling motion*. It is the same Greek word used in John 13:2 to depict that moment when the devil swiftly *injected* a seed of betrayal into Judas' heart. (You will see more about this in the next chapter.)

When the word *dia* and *balos* are used together, it forms the word *diabalos*, which is the New Testament word for the *devil*. It literally describes *one who repetitively hits something again and again and again — until finally that object is so worn down and defeated that it can be pierced and penetrated.*

An example of this in the natural realm would be the collective effect of water dripping on a rock. One little drop by itself isn't powerful, but when thousands of little water droplets drip *again, again, again,* and *again* over a prolonged period of time, the force of their combined dripping has the potential to drive a hole all the way through solid rock!

That's why you need to fortify yourself with the Word of God and surround yourself with people of faith, especially when you are tired and exhausted. The devil revels in attacking when you are in a weakened condition. He cherishes those moments when he finds you alone and worn out. When you are *fatigued, wiped out, drained,* and *sapped,* he knows that you are more susceptible to the lies and images he wants to feed you.

Daniel 7:25 explicitly tells us that the devil loves to "wear out the saints." He does this by continually feeding his cunning words of deception to our mind and emotions. His goal is to break down our resistance so he can fill our minds with accusatory assertions about ourselves or someone else.

Therefore, if you know you are in a weakened condition, you must be more watchful about thoughts that pass through your mind. When you are weak, tired, and worn out, it is much easier to see things *amiss*, to hear things *wrongly*, and to perceive things *incorrectly*.

I rarely have difficult conversations when I'm exhausted because that's one of those times when I don't see, hear, or perceive things well. I have seen the devil take advantage of these moments in my life too many times, arousing my temper and causing me to get agitated. Since I know this about myself, I try to stay out of intense conversations when I'm extremely tired and therefore more easily tempted by the devil. It's better for me and everyone else involved to wait until I have regained my strength.

Don't Give the Devil a Chance To Get In the Middle Of Your Relationships

So often we open the door for the devil and invite him right in by having quarrels and disagreements at moments when we are weak or tired. Sure, problems need to be discussed. But they *don't* need to be discussed when we're so exhausted, we can't see straight! That's one of those moments when we are *perfect prey* for the devil's attack!

Think for a moment. How many friendships could have been spared if everyone involved had taken a little time to rest before they expressed their disagreements and differences? How many marriages could have avoided ugly, debasing, tearing words if the husband and wife had gone separate ways for a couple of hours to pray and assess the situation before they continued their dialogue?

When *nonconstructive, pessimistic, disapproving, unhelpful, cynical, mocking, sarcastic,* and *disparaging* thoughts start to flood your mind about someone, it's best for you to back away from those thoughts for a while and give yourself a break. That string of negative feelings should be a warning flag to you that *the accuser* is trying to wedge his way into your mind and emotions.

When the mental attack starts, it may sound like this:

- *Why do you let those people treat you the way they do?*

- *They don't appreciate you, so why do you keep doing all the things you do for them?*

- *It would be better for you to go join another church where you'd be recognized and honored!*

- *Stop serving your ungrateful husband — he doesn't deserve someone as kind as you!*

If you don't turn a deaf ear to what the devil is telling you, it won't be long until those lies begin to sprout and send roots of bitterness deep inside your head and heart. And if you don't uproot and remove those lies, they'll soon affect your friendships and relationships.

A Relationship-Breaker From the Beginning of Time

The devil has tried to wedge his way between relationships from the very beginning of time.

First, he stirred up strife between one-third of the angels and God.

Second, he made his way into the Garden of Eden and tried to ruin the relationship between God and man.

Third, he wedged his way between Cain and Abel — two blood brothers — and succeeded in causing mankind's first murder.

From beginning to end, the Bible makes it clear that the devil has always been a *relationship-breaker*. Since that is the case, it is *imperative* that you learn how to protect yourself against his attacks.

Are Your Relationships a Joy or a Curse?

Relationships can be a *joy* or a *curse* in life, and you are the one who decides which they will be. Two key factors that determine the nature of your relationships are 1) how you nurture your relationships and 2) how you deal with conflict.

Most conflicts stem from petty disagreements that aren't even important. Oh, how the devil loves to uses unimportant clashes to destroy healthy relationships!

What makes it even worse is the fact that, while the fight is on and emotions are engaged, those who are arguing frequently can't even remember how the fight got started in the first place! *This should tell the parties involved how unimportant the conflict really is.*

These disruptions create tensions that rob us of our joy and make us nervous and sick from being upset all the time. That's why Jesus warned us, "The thief cometh not, but for to steal, and to kill, and to destroy…" (John 10:10).

Isn't It Time for You To Get Over It?

You see, the enemy wants to steal your fellowship, kill the sweet friendship you once had, and totally destroy any prospect of restoring that partnership. Don't let him do it! Use what you know about how he operates to stand against his wiles and deceptions and walk free of bitterness and strife!

In the next chapter, I want to show you how Satan penetrated one of Jesus' closest associates and friends. This chapter will help you understand how the devil used your friend or close associates to shove that knife so deep into your heart!

CHAPTER FOUR

Judas Iscariot – The Friend Who Became Jesus' Betrayer

Judas Iscariot was Jesus' close associate for three and a half years before he became a betrayer. In fact, he was so close to Jesus that John 12:6 says he became the treasurer for Jesus' ministry. This gives us insight into the kind of relationship that existed between Jesus and Judas.

We may assume that, as treasurer for Jesus' large ministry, Judas probably had many lengthy conversations with Him to discuss finances. Jesus must have trusted Judas and his administrative abilities to put him in charge of such a vital part of the ministry. *Yet this trusted friend and associate became the very one Satan used to betray Jesus.*

How Did One of Jesus' Disciples Become His Betrayer?

Have you ever wondered how it was possible for someone so close to Jesus to become His betrayer? *How did the devil slip through the cracks and so affect Judas' attitude that he would sell the Son of God for thirty pieces of silver?*

As we have already seen, the devil is looking for a way to penetrate every good relationship. No story demonstrates this better than the story of Judas Iscariot. Let's take a look at one particular event where the devil obviously found a point of penetration into Judas' life.

In John 12, Jesus and His disciples were having dinner in the home of Mary, Martha, and their brother Lazarus, whom Jesus had raised from the dead. This family was very close to Jesus during His earthly ministry.

Martha showed her love and gratitude for what Jesus had done for them by preparing a large meal for Him and His disciples. Mary showed her love by bringing Jesus an extremely expensive gift. Lazarus showed his love by simply sitting with Jesus at the table as a close friend. *This is an interesting demonstration of how different people express their love in different ways.*

Mary's Lavishly Expensive Gift

The Bible tells us that the expensive gift Mary brought Jesus was ointment of spikenard — an entire pound of it! Spikenard was one of the most expensive perfumes that existed at that time. Let me tell you a little about spikenard so you can appreciate what Mary did for Jesus that day.

Spikenard was an uncommon perfume extracted from grasses that grew in the country of India. Once the juices were squeezed out of the grass, they were dried into a hard, lardlike substance.

Turning that lardlike substance into perfume was a very lengthy and costly process. Add to this the cost of transporting it from India to other parts of the world, and you can see why this particular perfume cost so much money.

Spikenard was so expensive that few people could buy it; most had to buy one of the many cheap imitations available. But the word used in John 12:3 tells us that Mary didn't bring Jesus a cheap imitation; she brought Jesus the *real thing* — an ointment so valuable, it was normally reserved and used only as gifts for kings and nobility. *This was the gift Mary brought to Jesus.*

We can learn more about the value of Mary's gift in John 12:3, where it says the ointment was "very costly." This phrase "very costly" is from the Greek word *polutimos*, a compound of the words *polus* and *timios*.

The word *polus* means *much* or *great*. The word *timios* means *to honor*; *to respect*; or *worth*. Together, these words describe *something that is of great worth or something that is of considerable financial value.*

We'd call this "top-of-the-line giving"! As remarkable as it is that Mary even possessed a gift this valuable, it is even more amazing that she brought it to Jesus. *And even more phenomenal than that is what she did with this perfume once she brought it!*

Mary's Expression of Appreciation For Jesus

John 12:3 says, "Then took Mary a pound of ointment of spikenard, very costly, and anointed the feet of Jesus...." Everyone must have gasped when they saw Mary take the lid off that bottle, tip it downward, and begin to pour that precious ointment on Jesus' feet. This kind of perfume was not normally used on feet! Mary's action would have been considered a horrible *waste* in most people's minds, but that's not how she saw it. Mary *loved, appreciated,* and *valued* the feet of the Master!

Isn't It Time for You To Get Over It?

Isaiah 52:7 describes why Mary felt this way: "How beautiful upon the mountains are the feet of him that bringeth good tidings, that publisheth peace; that bringeth good tidings of good, that publisheth salvation; that saith unto Zion, Thy God reigneth!" No other feet in the entire world were more beautiful to Mary than the feet of Jesus. Jesus had changed her life and brought her brother back from the dead (*see* John 11:32-44). For her, every step Jesus took was *precious, honored,* and *greatly valued.*

For three and a half years, Jesus had taught, "For where your treasure is, there will your heart be also" (Matthew 6:21; Luke 12:34). Mary's actions revealed her heart as she poured her *most valuable treasure* onto the feet of Jesus.

John 12:3 tells us that she "...wiped his feet with her hair...." In other words, after Mary poured the spikenard onto Jesus' feet, she reached up to her head, untied her long, beautiful hair, and gathered it in her hands. Then she leaned down and began to wipe Jesus' feet dry with her hair.

In the days of the New Testament, a woman's hair represented her *glory* and *honor*. The apostle Paul referred to this in First Corinthians 11:15 when he wrote that a woman's hair was a "glory" to her.

For Mary to undo her hair and use it as a towel to wipe the feet of Jesus was probably the greatest act of humility she could have shown. She was demonstrating how deeply she loved and how greatly she valued Jesus.

I can imagine the tears that streamed down Mary's cheeks as she touched those precious feet. In total humility, she dried Jesus' feet with the glory and honor of her hair. John 12:3 tells us that "…the house was filled with the odour of the ointment."

An Opportunity For Bitterness, Resentment, and Offense

But then the devil used Mary's act of humility and love toward Jesus to create an opportunity for bitterness, resentment, and offense to take over in Judas' mind. Judas indignantly asked Jesus, "Why was not this ointment sold for three hundred pence, and given to the poor?" (John 12:5).

Judas said the spikenard could have been sold for "three hundred pence." What is a "pence"? The Greek word for a "pence" is *denarius*. In that day, a Roman *denarius* was *one day's salary*.

When Judas announced that the spikenard could have been sold for three hundred pence, he was saying that Mary's perfume was worth *300 days of salary*. In other words, this was an *extremely expensive gift*! But Jesus explained to Judas that Mary was anointing Him for the day of His burial. He also told Judas to leave Mary alone and not to disturb what she was doing (*see* John 12:7).

Jesus' Words Could Have Offended Anyone Listening

Then Jesus continued, saying, "For the poor always ye have with you; but me ye have not always" (John 12:8).

This answer could have easily been misinterpreted! Those who were listening could have thought Jesus was saying, "Quit talking about poor people! You'll always have the poor, but you won't always have *Me*!"

Jesus had certainly demonstrated His compassion toward the poor during His three years of ministry. Nevertheless, His words to Judas could have sounded *arrogant* and *insensitive* to those who were listening.

Did Judas misinterpret Jesus' response that evening? Did he perceive Jesus to be arrogant and insensitive to the needs of poor people?

The disciples watched as this valued treasure was poured out on Jesus' feet. It looked like superfluous waste and excess. It is obvious that Judas considered it to be exactly that.

What about all the poor people who could have been helped with the money from the sale of that perfume? *Weren't they more important than this demonstration of love that cost so much?*

As you will see in John 13:2, the devil found entrance into Judas' heart during this dinner at the home of Martha, Mary, and Lazarus. Somehow that evening the enemy had found an open door — a way to penetrate Judas' mind.

How Did the Devil Get a Foothold In the Mind and Heart of Judas?

How did the devil get inside Jesus' inner circle of friends to try to abort his ministry? Did Judas become *offended* with Jesus? Is this how the devil started pounding away at Judas' mind until he was finally lured into betraying Jesus?

Judas Iscariot – The Friend Who Became Jesus' Betrayer

John 13:2 tells us something *very powerful* about the way the devil established a foothold in Judas' heart and mind that night. It says, "And supper being ended, the devil having now *put into* the heart of Judas Iscariot, Simon's son, to betray him."

Especially notice the phrase, "…the devil having now put into the heart of Judas Iscariot…." The words "put into" come from the Greek word *ballo*, which means *to throw, to cast, to thrust, or to inject*. This word *ballo* carries the idea of *a very fast action of throwing, thrusting, or injecting something forward — perhaps like the throwing of a ball or rock or the forward thrusting of a sharp knife.*

I want to give you some examples of the word *ballo* in the New Testament. Look carefully at how the word *ballo* is used in each of these various references.

Isn't It Time for You To Get Over It?

1. Matthew 9:17; Mark 2:22; Luke 5:37

The word *ballo* is used in these verses to depict *putting wine into new wineskins*. The emphasis is on *putting wine into a new bottle or making a deposit into a receptacle.*

2. Matthew 25:27

The word *ballo* is used to depict *putting money into the hands of investors or depositing money into a place that will earn interest for the investor.*

3. Matthew 27:6

The word *ballo* is used to depict *putting or depositing money into the treasury or bank*. Again, the emphasis is on *making a deposit*.

4. Mark 7:33

The word *ballo* is used to depict *Jesus putting His fingers into the ears of a deaf man*.

Because this word *ballo* is used, it tells us Jesus didn't take a lot of time to tell the deaf man what He was about to do. Instead, He *abruptly inserted* His fingers into the man's ears to initiate the man's healing.

5. John 5:7

The word *ballo* is used when the crippled man states *he has no one to put him into the pool when the water is stirred.* Here the word *ballo* means *to cast, to throw, to forcibly hurl the crippled man forward into the pool so quickly that he gets in before anyone else.*

6. John 12:6

The word *ballo* is used to describe *Judas' responsibility for the money that was put into the bag or the treasury of Jesus' ministry.* The force of the word *ballo* indicates *a deposit made so deep that it isn't retractable.* As treasurer, Judas alone had the authority to remove the money once it had been *deposited* into the bag.

7. John 18:11

The word *ballo* is used when *Jesus commands Peter to put his sword back into its sheath in the Garden of Gethsemane.* The use of the word *ballo* indicates Jesus *abruptly* commanded Peter to *put* his sword away and to do it *quickly*.

8. John 20:25

The word *ballo* is used when Thomas says *he must put, thrust, or insert his fingers into the nail prints of Jesus' hands, feet, and side in order to believe.* The primary idea of *ballo* in this verse is to *insert into* or *to thrust into*.

In all these examples, the word *ballo* carries the idea of *quickly inserting, injecting, thrusting, putting into, forcibly hurling, or deeply embedding something into an object*. The usage of this word tells us that when the devil decided to "put into" the heart of Judas the idea of betraying Jesus, he knew he had to *act fast*.

When Satan finally penetrated Judas' mind and emotions with this seed of betrayal, he injected it so hard and fast that it became *deeply embedded* or *lodged* in Judas' soul. Therefore, John 13:2 could be translated:

- *"...the devil having now thrust into...."*

- *"...the devil having now inserted into...."*

- *"...the devil having now forcibly hurled into...."*

- *"...the devil having now embedded into...."*

There is no doubt that the word *ballo* means the devil *quickly seized* an opportunity and *injected* a seed of betrayal into the heart of Judas Iscariot. Judas was so offended by Jesus' statement about the poor that a window to his heart and emotions was opened. That was the moment the devil found his entrance into Judas' heart. At last, Satan had found a way to penetrate into Jesus' inner circle!

Judas was used as Satan's instrument because he allowed the enemy to drive a wedge between him and Jesus. Rather than let the disagreement go and forget about it, Judas allowed the issue to become a big deal in his mind — something blown all out of proportion. He let the devil mess around in his mind and emotions and didn't take every thought captive; as a result, the incident tainted his view of Jesus and affected their relationship.

Has this ever happened to you?

- *Have you ever had moments when you were tempted to think badly of someone?*

- *Did you know that at that moment, you faced a choice — you could either overlook what the person had done to offend you, or you could let the offense get lodged deep down inside you?*

- *Were you aware that the devil was trying to sow a seed of discord into your soul?*

- *Were you conscious that the enemy was attempting to make you get offended or upset?*

- *Have you experienced times when the devil's plan worked because you made the wrong choice, allowing your mind to be seized by bitter, resentful thoughts?*

Well, that is exactly what happened to Judas Iscariot.

When Satan Tried To Use Me As a Betrayer

I'll never forget the time in my life when Satan tried to use me as a betrayer. I was a young man, working as an associate pastor in a large Southern Baptist church. The pastor I assisted was a wonderful man who had taught me and unselfishly given his life to me. He loved me as if I were his own son.

Then one day, I became *offended* by something this pastor did. (You can read more of this testimony in my book, *Who Is Ready for a Spiritual Promotion?*)

In retrospect, I see that what happened was minor and shouldn't have affected me at all. (Isn't it amazing how well we all see things in *retrospect?*) But the devil had been waiting for the perfect opportunity to attack my mind and try to ruin our relationship. At that moment, I was his *perfect prey*. The incident that had offended me became a major issue in my mind. I didn't realize that I was allowing this *overexaggerated issue* to become an open door for the devil.

It is amazing how quickly a dart of the enemy can be thrown into your heart. Equally amazing is the speed with which just one of his evil darts can change your perspective of someone you used to honor and respect!

Judas Iscariot – The Friend
Who Became Jesus' Betrayer

In a matter of *seconds,* my entire view of this man had become adversely affected. Like the dripping of the water I wrote about earlier, the devil began to repeatedly strike my mind with accusations against that pastor. The enemy would whisper to my mind:

- *He is so arrogant and proud!*

- *If other people saw what you see, no one would attend this church. He doesn't really love his people!*

- *He doesn't appreciate you. He doesn't deserve to have you serve on his staff. Leave him!*

- *The people in this city need a pastor who really loves them. It's time for you to leave him and go start your own church!*

I didn't realize that deception was creeping into my heart. I myself had fallen into the devil's trap and didn't know it. What I ended up doing to that pastor was blatantly wrong. However, at the moment it was happening, I *really* believed I was doing the right thing.

Questions To Ask When Something Is Becoming a Major Issue to You

Whenever something becomes a *major issue* between you and someone else, you would be wise to back up and reexamine what you are upset about. So often the person you are upset with is someone you love and need in your life. Therefore, ask yourself these questions:

- *Do I want to let the devil build a wall between me and that other person over something that won't even matter one or two years from now?*

- *Do I really think that person intended to hurt me?*

- *Wouldn't it be better to forgive that person and preserve our relationship that has taken so long to build?*

- *Is what happened really so serious, or am I blowing the whole incident out of proportion?*

- *Have I ever been guilty of doing the same thing to someone else?*

I have discovered from my own experience that the devil is constantly seeking opportune moments to wedge bad feelings between people. He is a master at embellishing real or imagined offenses in your mind until they become inflated and larger than life. And he knows just when to sock it to you!

It's Time To Make An Examination of Your Heart

Now let me give an important piece of advice: If you will concentrate your attention on the condition of your own heart, it will give you less time to nit-pick about what you *think* is happening in everyone else's heart!

Isn't It Time for You To Get Over It?

The condition of our hearts is serious business! Hebrews 12:15 tells us that it is our responsibility to oversee what goes on inside our own hearts, minds, and emotions. As long as our hearts and minds are free of bitterness, resentment, and unforgiveness, the enemy will find it harder to penetrate us or to access our relationships. We don't ever have to make the mistake Judas did!

CHAPTER FIVE

You Are the Bishop Of Your Own Heart

Now let's take a look at Hebrews 12:15 to see what it says about *bitterness, resentment,* and *unforgiveness.* How do we *uproot* and *remove* these devilish "weeds" from our lives?

Hebrews 12:15 tells us, "Looking diligently lest any man fail of the grace of God; lest any root of bitterness springing up trouble you, and thereby many be defiled." I want you to especially notice the words "looking diligently" in this verse.

This phrase comes from the Greek word *episkopos,* taken from the two words *epi* and *skopos*. The word *epi* means *over*, and the word *skopos* means *to look*. When these two words are compounded into one word as in Hebrews 12:15, the word means *to look over* or *to take supervisory oversight*.

The word *episkopos* is the same Greek word translated "bishop" in First Timothy 3:1. As you know, a bishop has *oversight* or *responsibility* for a group of churches. As the chief overseer for those churches, it is the bishop's responsibility to *watch, direct, guide, correct,* and *give oversight* to the churches under his care. As long as he serves as bishop, he will be held responsible for the *good* and the *bad* that occurs under his ministry.

Hebrews 12:15 uses the word *episkopos* to alert you and me to the fact that *we are the bishops of our own hearts*. The use of this word in this verse means it is our responsibility to *watch, direct, guide, correct,* and *give oversight* to what goes on inside us.

You Are the Bishop Of Your Own Heart

As the bishop of your own heart:

- *It is your responsibility to guide, direct, and give oversight to what goes on inside your emotions and thinking.*

- *You alone are responsible for what you allow to develop inside your head and heart.*

- *Like a bishop, you are personally responsible for both the good and the bad that occurs within your thought life.*

Why do I make this point? Because we are often tempted to blame our *bad attitudes, bitterness, resentments, or feelings of unforgiveness* on other people. But the truth is, we are responsible for our own emotions and reactions!

If a person does something that has the potential to offend us, God holds *us* responsible for whether or not that offense takes root in our minds. We can choose to let it sink into our souls and take root, or we can opt to let it bypass us. We are not able to control what others do or say to us, but we *are* able to control what goes on *inside* of us.

It is that "inside" part — *the part we control* — that God will hold us responsible for. Why? Because we are charged with a personal responsibility to oversee what goes on inside our souls.

You have the last word. You are the one who decides whether or not that wrong settles down into your soul and starts to take root in your emotions.

You may say, *"But, Rick, what that other person did to me was so wrong. It hurt me so deeply! It made me so mad!"*

Anger is an emotion that comes and goes. You *choose* whether or not irritation turns into *anger*, anger into *wrath*, wrath into *bitterness*, bitterness into *resentment*, and resentment into *unforgiveness*. You *choose* whether these foul attitudes and emotions take up residency in your heart or are booted out the door!

When the devil comes to tempt you with an annoying, hounding thought about the person who offended you, at that moment you have a choice whether or not to let it sink in. You are the *only* one who can give permission for these attitudes to make their habitation in your mind and emotions.

So quit saying, "I'm this way because So-and-so did this to me" or "I can't help the way I feel." *Those are all lies.*

If you're filled with *bitterness*, *resentment*, and *unforgiveness*, the reason is that you *permitted* the devil to sow that destructive seed in your heart and then you *permitted* it to grow. Remember, you're the bishop of your own heart!

Keep the Weeds Out of Your Own 'Garden'

There is only one reason weeds grow out of control in a garden — because no one took the proper time and care to uproot and remove them.

Isn't It Time for You To Get Over It?

When the garden is choked by weeds, the gardener can't complain, "I just don't know how this happened! How did this occur right under my nose?" It occurred because he was being irresponsible with his garden. If he'd been exercising the proper amount of diligence, he would have known that weeds were about to get the best of him. His *lack of diligence* is the reason his garden got into this mess!

Hebrews 12:15 says, "Looking *diligently*...." It takes *diligence* to keep your heart in good shape. The only way you can stay free of the weeds the devil wants to sow in your "garden" is to be attentive, careful, thorough, and meticulous about the condition of your own heart.

Don't expect others to take care of your heart for you either. It's *your* heart!

Also, don't make excuses for the rotten attitudes that fill your thoughts about people who supposedly did you wrong. Even if they really did commit a wrong against you, was it necessary or beneficial to permit the devil to fill you with putrid feelings of bitterness, resentment, and unforgiveness? Get over it! What good does it do to let the offense fester inside you until you are inwardly eaten up by its bad memory?

As long as you blame everyone else for the bitterness that rages inside, you'll never walk free. If you're going to get over the offense and walk free of your emotional prison, you must start by accepting responsibility for your own heart.

- *You are the bishop of your own heart.*

- *You are responsible for what materializes inside your heart.*

- *You are the only one with the authority to permit bitterness, resentment, and unforgiveness to take root and grow in your heart.*

- *You have the power of the Holy Spirit at your disposal to uproot and remove those spiritual weeds — IF you really want them removed!*

- *You cannot escape personal responsibility for the attitudes you carry inside about other people.*

God Holds Us All Responsible

If someone deliberately sows bad seeds in our "garden" in an effort to hurt or destroy us, *God will deal with them.* But if we know bad seed is sown in our hearts and we just ignore it, allowing it to take root and grow unchecked, *God will deal with us.*

- *God will hold others responsible for what they do to us.*

- *God will hold US responsible for what we allow to go on inside our minds and hearts.*

- *We cannot answer for the actions of other people.*

- *We will answer for our inward responses to what others have done to us.*

Let me give you an example from my own life that occurred many years ago. I'll never forget an experience I had with a brother in the Lord who *deliberately* tried to injure our ministry.

To this day, I don't understand why this man did what he did — and in retrospect, I don't think he knows why he did it either. But what he did at that time was very hurtful to the outreach of our work, and the devil tried to use his actions to make me *bitter*. When it happened, I knew I had to make a choice *to forgive or to hold on to the offense.*

The more I thought about what the man did, the more upset I became. Soon my negative feelings toward him grew deeper and deeper into my soul. My thoughts toward him were bitter — and these unchecked thoughts began to affect my spiritual life. I smiled and spoke politely to him when in a situation that demanded I speak to him, but inwardly I *resented* him with every bone of my body.

The devil began pounding my mind. I knew it was the devil, but I was so "ticked off" at what the man had done to us that I allowed every negative word and imagination to freely pass through my mind. Even worse, I allowed *agreement* to rise from my soul about everything the devil said about him.

After allowing these devilish thoughts to have free course in my mind for a while, I came to the place where this man *disgusted* me. The very thought of him perturbed me. As far as I was concerned, he was a *no-good, low-down, useless bum* parading about in the disguise of a brother and man of God. When others spoke highly of him, it irritated me. I wanted everyone to know the *truth* as I knew it! I wanted people to know what a *wretch* he was!

I found my mind dominated by this man and what he had done to us. Denise pleaded with me to give the matter to the Lord, but I told her,

"He's done us wrong, and I have every right to feel the way I do."

I knew I was in deep water spiritually when I asked God to take the man's life and deliver me from having to deal with him ever again! But that man was no longer the problem! *I was the problem!*

I was filled with bitterness because I had chosen to let bitterness have a place inside me. God's way was forgiveness, but I had *permitted* and even *cultivated* my offended feelings toward this brother because of what he had done to me.

- *I knew I needed to forgive.*

- *I knew I needed to let go of the offense and let it die.*

- *I knew I was filled with a wrong attitude.*

- *I knew I was hurting myself more than I was hurting anyone else.*

- *I knew my feelings of hostility weren't healthy.*

- *I even knew my flesh was throwing a pity party in the midst of trying to justify my wretched feelings about this man.*

I was overflowing with anger and resentment for what the man had done. Because of this, I was in no position to stand in judgment of someone else. What he had done couldn't have been any worse than the ungodly emotions I was now harboring against him. His sinful actions were outward, to be seen by all. On the other hand, mine were inward and hidden, and they were tearing me up on the inside!

One day the Lord spoke to me, saying, "Rick, I'm going to hold you responsible for the bitterness you've allowed to work in your heart toward this man. Yes, what he did was wrong — *and I will deal with that*. But if you don't deal with your own heart and get rid of this bitterness toward your brother, *I will deal with you!*"

Stay Out of the Judgment Business

Regardless of what that brother had done to me, I knew that bitterness and offense were *not* to have a place in my heart. Neither was it my place to "play God" and decide who needed to be judged.

Our flesh is always tempted to judge others for their failures. *But judgment is not our business.* It is God's place to decide whose actions and motivations are right or wrong — *not ours.* When we move ourselves into a position of deciding whose motives are right or wrong, we have assumed a responsibility that does *not* belong to us. According to Romans 12:19, it is *God's business* to deal with those who have done us wrong, not ours. We aren't even supposed to touch it!

The longer I've walked with the Lord, the more I've come to realize how difficult it is to figure out my own heart, let alone everyone else's hearts as well! In this particular case, it was *my* heart that was filled with a root of bitterness; therefore, I needed to deal with *myself*. No one could make that choice for me. God's Spirit made it very clear that it was my responsibility to uproot and remove that garbage from my soul. God would empower me to do it, *but He wouldn't do it without my cooperation.*

This is a very important principle for you to understand.

We are all occasionally tempted to become bitter or offended with husbands, wives, siblings, parents, and brothers or sisters in the Lord. *But we must understand that offense is a killer of our spiritual lives.*

I understand that it's disappointing when your husband is harsh, unkind, and inconsiderate. It's frustrating when your wife nags at you all the time. It's hurtful when your children are disrespectful and rebellious. It's a disappointment when your friends aren't there when you need them. It's agonizing when a person fails you. It's heartbreaking when you put your whole heart into a relationship and it doesn't turn out the way you hoped. It's devastating when someone else gets the promotion you have been waiting to receive.

But rather than let the devil use these adversities to fill us with *bitterness, resentment,* and *unforgiveness*, we must do everything we can to forgive, forget, and keep our hearts free! Rather than blame what we feel on others, we must take personal responsibility for our thoughts and uproot offense from our souls before it produces destruction in our spiritual lives.

God's Spirit will speak to your heart and warn you to deal with bitterness before it becomes deeply rooted in your soul. This divine pleading is *God's grace* trying to help you overcome the situation before it becomes more serious. Don't ignore that grace!

Let God's Grace Help You!

Whether or not you live free from bitterness and unforgiveness depends on your *willingness* to let God direct your life and change what's wrong in your thinking. God in His grace wants to help you, but He *can't* help you if you won't listen or if you refuse to do what the Word tells you. Your cooperation is *required* in order for God's grace to accomplish its full work inside you.

When the Holy Spirit speaks to your heart about letting an offense go, it is *God's grace* trying to help you forgive what your offender has done. God wants to deliver you from bitterness and resentment before you sink so deeply into Satan's trap that it becomes extremely difficult for you to get out of it.

So listen to the Holy Spirit, and allow His grace to have its full effect in your life. Then bitterness and resentment won't have an opportunity to become rooted so deeply inside your heart!

- *You know the Holy Spirit's voice.*

- *You know when He's telling you to forgive.*

- *You know when God's grace is trying to help you.*

If you'll just do what God is telling you to do, you'll be spared from the aches and pains that come with bitterness, resentment, and unforgiveness. But if you choose to hold on to those destructive feelings and *ignore* what God is trying to do to help you overcome, you will fall short the grace of God. That's exactly what Hebrews 12:15 is talking about when it says, "Looking diligently, *lest any man fail of the grace of God....*"

We once had a woman in our church who had suffered many rejections during her lifetime. She had been rejected by her mother, her father, her husband, and even by her children.

When God first brought this woman to our church, we knew He had brought her to us for her full restoration. *God's grace* was on her in a powerful way to bring her to a place of personal change and of forgiveness toward those who had offended her through the years.

Day by day she'd come closer and closer to forgiveness. Then something would happen that would trigger her old feelings of bitterness. *God's grace* was there to help this woman overcome those bitter feelings, but time after time she rejected that grace and reached back to grab hold of that bitterness again. I am amazed at the incredible grace that was available to help her change — *but she rejected it over and over again.*

Today the woman still attends church, but she is not a free person. She still carries the same old deep scars she has always carried. It isn't that *God's grace* wasn't available to change her. Divine grace was mightily available, but she didn't allow it to work; therefore, *she failed the grace of God.*

Don't let that be your story. You are the personal caretaker of your own heart, and God will hold you responsible for the attitudes that linger inside you. God's grace is available to help you change. You don't have to be imprisoned in bitterness, unforgiveness, or resentment any longer.

If these destructive inward feelings have established a stronghold in your life, make the choice to reach out and grab hold of God's grace. His grace will break those chains off your soul and set you free from the prison of offense that has held you captive for so long!

You Have No Excuses To Stay the Way You Are

You know, all of us may have *reasons* why we harbor ill feelings toward someone, but as caretakers of our own hearts, we have *no excuses* for holding on to those ill feelings.

God's Spirit wants to give you 1) freedom from the offense that was done to you and 2) freedom to forgive the person or group of people who offended you. But in order to experience that freedom, you have to recognize that:

- We've all been offended by someone at some point in our lives.

- We've all been guilty of offending someone else at some point in our lives.

- We all exhibit a bad memory when we say to someone else, *"How dare you do that to me!"*

If you stopped and thought for just a few minutes, you'd probably remember a time when you committed the same offense against someone else that has been committed against you. You may be upset about what that person did to you. *But is it possible you are reaping something you have sown?*

Before you get angry with the other person, you need to look at yourself and ask if you're experiencing the law of sowing and reaping (Galatians 6:7). It may be difficult to admit to yourself, but often it's the truth.

When I am tempted to get upset with people who are unfaithful to me in our ministry, the Holy Spirit reminds me of times when I was younger and I was unfaithful to those who were over *me*.

Remembering my past mistakes helps me overlook and forgive the mistakes of others. It also brings repentance to my heart for the times I have done others wrong with my own actions or lack of actions.

I may have a *reason* to be upset with someone, but I have no excuse to stay upset, especially when I remember how much mercy has been shown to me in the past for stupid mistakes and foolish statements I've unintentionally made. *How can anyone who has been shown as much mercy as I have been shown judge others who have made the same mistakes?*

How's Your Memory Working?

We usually become judgmental and unforgiving when we are so focused on what was done to *us* that we forget what we have done to *others* in the past. The truth is, we've probably been guilty in the past of the very offense we're so upset about right now!

Isn't It Time for You To Get Over It?

We all make mistakes. We all say stupid things we later regret. We all do things, whether right or wrong, that are misunderstood by others. We've all done things that we thought were right at the moment, only to realize later how wrong we were in our actions and attitudes.

Until Christians have glorified bodies and are in Heaven, they must deal with their own inconsistencies and blemishes. Even those who spend ten hours a day in prayer make mistakes that remind them that they are made of dust (Psalm 103:14).

When I deal with staff members who are upset with each other, I remind them of Romans 15:7. It says, "Wherefore receive ye one another, as Christ also received us to the glory of God."

• How did Christ receive you?

He received you freely — with no strings attached.

- What condition were you in when He saved you?

You were an ugly mess.

- Have you made any mistakes since you were saved?

Absolutely yes!

- Have you ever disappointed the Lord since you've been saved?

Yes, absolutely yes!

- Does Jesus still love you, accept you, and work with you in spite of your hang-ups?

Thank God, YES!

Romans 15:7 says that this is *exactly* how we are to receive one another. Certainly we must deal with problems when they occur. Yes, we must be honest about the things that bother us. But we should never allow an issue to become so big that it separates us from each other.

Isn't It Time for You To Get Over It?

Think of all the things YOU'VE done to the Lord that you would never tolerate if someone else did them to you. Yet He has never turned from you and is still patiently working with you all the time!

The devil has been able to destroy so many relationships because someone refused to be merciful and overlook an offense that he was probably guilty of himself at an earlier time. *Don't let that someone be you.* It is *crucial* for you to deal with bitterness, resentment, and unforgiveness *before* they get rooted deep down inside your mind and emotions.

- *Don't allow these attitudes to fester and get worse on the inside.*

- *Don't allow a judgmental spirit to take root inside you.*

The longer you let bitterness grow in your mind and emotions, the harder it will be to uproot and remove. You need to "lay the axe to the root" and *permanently remove* all bitterness before it adversely affects you and your relationship with the person or persons who committed the offense. *Whatever it takes, be a faithful bishop of your own heart!*

CHAPTER SIX

What Is A 'Root of Bitterness'?

In order to effectively "lay your axe" to the root of bitterness, you need to first understand how dangerous it is to you and to those around you. Let's look again at what Hebrews 12:15 says about it: "Looking diligently lest any man fail of the grace of God; lest any root of bitterness springing up trouble you, and thereby many be defiled."

The word "root" is the Greek word *pidzo*. It refers to *a root, such as the root of a tree*. These are *roots that have gone down deep and are now deeply embedded*. Therefore, the word *pidzo* often denotes *something that is established or firmly fixed*.

If bitterness becomes *deeply embedded* in your soul against a person, your negative opinion of that person will become *firmly fixed*. As time passes, your thoughts of judgment against him will become more developed, rationalized, and established. That root of bitterness will become so firmly fixed inside of you that your angry, judgmental thoughts about the person will actually begin to make sense to you.

When a "root of bitterness" gets this *deeply embedded* in your mind and emotions, it's no longer just a "root" you're dealing with; now you have a *mental stronghold*. That stronghold of bitterness will take a lofty position in your mind and emotions. From that position, it will then present a myriad of logical reasons why you shouldn't have anything else to do with that person and why you should keep your distance from him.

The word "bitterness" comes from the Greek word *pikria*. It refers to *an inward attitude that is*

What Is A 'Root of Bitterness'?

so bitter, it produces a scowl on one's face. In other words, you become so inwardly *infected* with bitterness that you are outwardly *affected* in your appearance and disposition.

This "bitterness" is acid to one's soul, and eventually it begins to surface. When it does, the fruit it produces is *unkind, sour, sharp, sarcastic, scornful, cynical, mocking, contemptuous,* and *wounding.* Bitterness has nothing good to say about the other person. In fact, it looks for negative things to say about that person to affect others' opinions about him as well.

Tell-Tale Signs That Bitterness Is Growing in Your Life

When you find yourself constantly saying something derogatory about someone else, pay attention to what's happening! What you're saying about that person is a *tell-tale sign* that some bad seed is trying to take root in your heart.

Isn't It Time for You To Get Over It?

Hebrews 12:15 tells us how to recognize when bad seed is beginning to produce destructive fruit in our lives. It says, "...lest any root of bitterness *springing up* trouble you...." The words "springing up" are from the Greek word *phuoo*. This word depicts *a little plant that is just starting to sprout and grow*. It isn't a large plant yet; rather, it's a small seedling that is just breaking through the soil and starting to peek out at life. However, the very fact that it's peeking through the soil means there is a seed hidden in the soil producing this new life.

This is a very significant picture. It tells us that bitterness doesn't overwhelm us all at once. Instead, it grows a little here and a little there until it finally becomes a huge, ugly growth that defiles our entire lives.

Bitterness usually starts peeking up out of the depths of our souls in the form of negative thoughts about another person or a sour, sharp, distrusting, cynical attitude toward someone. If the root is not quickly uprooted and removed,

What Is
A 'Root of Bitterness'?

that bitterness will eventually become a full-blown tree that produces *bitter, wounding, hurtful,* and *scornful* fruit for everyone who eats of it.

As bad as this fruit is for others, it hurts no one more than it does you. Think for a moment about the woman I told you about in Chapter Five who lives in an emotional prison of unforgiveness. The people she despises have moved on with their lives, but she has remained *paralyzed* and *dysfunctional* behind those walls of offense and resentment.

Hebrews 12:15 shouts its warning: If you don't stop these attitudes, they will eventually "trouble you." The words "trouble you" are from the Greek word *enochleo*, which means *to trouble, to harass,* or *to annoy*. It refers to *something inside that bothers and upsets you so much, you are constantly pestered by thoughts about it*. In fact, your whole life is *stalk*ed by these *hassling, teasing thoughts*. What you allowed to take root and fester inside your soul now has become a *major nuisance* to your peace that keeps you upset and emotionally torn up all the time.

Let me put it to you this way:

- *Do you have a grudge against someone that just gnaws away at you all the time?*

- *Every time you see that person, do you feel something sharp and ugly inside?*

- *When you hear about that person being blessed, do you wonder how God could possibly bless him when he did such an ugly thing to you?*

- *Do negative thoughts like these pester and bother you all the time?*

If you relate to the situation I just described, watch out! Bitterness, resentment, and unforgiveness are now *hounding* and *stalking* you! These foul attitudes are hassling *you* more than they are bothering anyone else.

What Is
A 'Root of Bitterness'?

The very thought of the person who offended you *troubles, harasses* and *annoys* you. Yet that person is probably unaffected by your inward struggle; instead, he or she moves on in life while you wallow in unforgiveness! If this fact "gets your goat," then Hebrews 12:15 is describing *you* when it says, "…lest any root of bitterness springing up trouble you…."

If you don't get a grip on yourself right now and let the Holy Spirit help you permanently put these feelings aside, you'll fulfill the next part of the verse as well that says, "…and thereby many be *defiled.*"

Be Careful What You Dump On People Who Are Listening to You!

The word "defiled" is the Greek word *miaini*. It means *to spill, to spot,* or *to stain*. Think of what would happen if you spilled a glass of grape juice on white carpet. That beautiful carpet would be *stained* and *spotted* because of what you *dumped* on it, and a perfectly good carpet would be ruined.

What a powerful picture this is for you and me! It tells us that when we begin to "run at the mouth" and say bad things about someone else, we have a devastating effect on the listeners' attitudes. As our root of bitterness rages out of control, our derogatory words *taint, spot, soil,* and *ruin* the way those who listen perceive the person we are speaking of.

Previously our listeners may have held a high opinion of the person we're talking about. But by the time we're finished ranting and raving and expressing our bitterness (which may be dressed in a variety of disguises), we have completely soured their opinion of that person. They have been *spotted* by what we *dumped* on them.

An example would be a father who has always loved his church — until something happens in the church that offends him. Rather than release the offense and forgive, he goes home and *fumes* about what happened. The longer he fumes

What Is A 'Root of Bitterness'?

about it, the more angry he gets. As his anger grows, he starts venting and talking about what he thinks and feels. He is so *upset* with that church!

Previous to this moment, his children loved their church. They *thought* their father loved it too. But day after day, they listen to their father rage about how bad the pastor is or how badly he has been treated. He doesn't realize that his words are affecting his children.

Soon *the children* begin to feel what *their father* feels. They see what *he* sees and believe what *he* believes. It isn't too long before they are carrying the same bitter feelings toward the church as their father — even though nothing wrong has ever been done to them!

These children have been *tainted*, *stained*, and *spotted* by a father who should have kept his mouth shut, gone to the Cross, and allowed the Spirit of God to liberate him from those bitter emotions. Instead, he dumped his bitterness on his family.

Now the father is not the only one who has an attitude problem; he has imparted his bad attitude to his children as well. And if his children have a negative attitude toward the church when they grow up, much of the blame will be laid at that father's feet for not keeping his mouth shut and being more mature.

When a root of bitterness is not *uprooted* and *removed* by God's Spirit, it doesn't just affect you; it affects a lot of other people as well. Ultimately, it has the power to affect every friend or relative in your life.

What a pity to *dump* all your negative garbage on your friends and loved ones, defiling them with a spiritual problem that may hound them for years. *How much better it would be for you to go to the Cross and deal with it as a mature person than to sow a lot of bad seed you'll end up reaping later!*

What Is A 'Root of Bitterness'?

You *Will* Have an Opportunity To Get Offended!

In Luke 17:1, Jesus said, "...It is impossible but that offences will come...." The word "offense" is from the Greek word *skandalos*, from which we get the word *scandal*. *Skandalos* refers to *something that causes you to trip, to fall, or to stumble*. It has been translated *a stumbling block* or *a stumbling stone*.

But in plainer language, what is an *offense*? An *offense* occurs when you see, hear, or experience a behavior that is so different from what you expected that it causes you to *falter, totter,* and *wobble* in your soul and leaves you *reeling* on the inside. In fact, you just about *lose your footing* when this event occurs because it takes you so off guard. Now your opinion of that person you once admired has become *adversely affected*.

We've all experienced this kind of disappointment at some point in our lives. According to Jesus' teaching in Luke 17:1, the opportunity to be offended comes to every one of us. As long as we live and breathe, we must combat offense and *refuse* to allow it to have a place in our hearts and minds.

Even worse, we've all been the *source* of offense at one point or another. The offense may have been unintentional on our part; we may not have even known we offended anyone until the person came and informed us that he or she was upset. But regardless of intent, someone became offended by something we did or didn't do.

- *Have you ever offended someone?*

- *When you found out about it, were you shocked?*

- *When the news finally reached you that you had offended that person, were you surprised to hear how he or she perceived what you did or said?*

This happens to everyone. Through the years, I've learned to do the best I can to avoid being a

What Is A 'Root of Bitterness'?

source of offense to anyone. At the same time, I try not to be too shocked if I find out that someone, somewhere, has gotten offended.

Because people come from different backgrounds, wake up in different moods, and go through a host of different experiences in their lives, their interpretation of your actions and words may frequently be very different from what you intended. You can be almost 99% certain that someone along the way will misunderstand what you do or misinterpret something you say.

So often the hidden root of wars, family divisions, broken friendships, dissolved marriages, divided churches, and so on, can be found in the tangled mess of:

- *Misperceptions*

- *Misunderstandings*

- *Misinterpretations*

- *Misreadings*

- *Misconceptions*

- *Mistaken motives*

As Christians, we must 1) do everything in our power to *communicate correct messages* to one another; and 2) do everything in our power *to bring healing and forgiveness* whenever misunderstanding and offense occurs between ourselves and others.

If you discover you have been a source of offense to someone, *take the mature path and go ask for forgiveness.* Don't get defensive; that only makes the problem worse and often leads to an argument!

Ask for forgiveness, *even if you think you were never wrong in the first place.* Do everything you can to bury that offense and destroy what the devil is trying to do. Make it your personal aim to help that other person overcome what he *thinks* you did or said. Helping the other person attain a position of peace is more important than proving who is right or wrong.

What Is A 'Root of Bitterness'?

What if *You* Are the Offended One?

In Luke 17:3 and 4, Jesus said, "...If thy brother trespass against thee, rebuke him; and if he repent, forgive him. And if he trespass against thee seven times in a day, and seven times in a day turn again to thee, saying, I repent; thou shalt forgive him."

Jesus taught that if a brother or sister does something that you perceive to be wrong, *you are to go talk to the person about it.* If he or she apologizes and repents of his or her actions, *you are to forgive that person and let go of the offense.* If it's difficult for you to do that, you need to go to the Cross and ask the Holy Spirit to help you do it.

Walking in forgiveness is part of your lifestyle as a mature believer. Besides, hasn't the Lord forgiven you many times for sins you have committed against Him? How often has He forgiven you for doing the same thing again and again? If you've *received* this kind of mercy, isn't it right that you should *give* the same mercy to others?

When the disciples heard Jesus' teaching about forgiveness, they said to the Lord, "…Increase our faith" (Luke 17:5). That was the equivalent of saying, *"Lord, what You've just asked us to do is very hard! You've got to increase our faith and help us believe we can forgive so many times!"*

The truth is, God has already given you all the faith you need to forgive others when they offend or hurt you. But you still have to make the decision to *use* that faith to uproot every root of bitterness while it's still a little seedling. Don't wait to "lay the axe to the root" until you have a huge tree of anger and bitterness defiling your life!

CHAPTER SEVEN

It's Time for You To Let It Go!

It is difficult for most people to confront someone else regarding an offense, but sometimes confrontation is necessary. In fact, ignoring confrontation is often what causes bad feelings to turn inward and fester into something much worse. Those ugly feelings can sit in the pit of a person's stomach, churning and churning away, until he becomes so upset that he can hardly see straight.

Usually it's better to kindly say what you feel and get over it than to let those raw emotions turn into an ugly monster, just waiting to crawl out at an opportune moment and attack its victim. That is frequently what happens when you allow ugly emotions to go unchecked. Confrontation may be uneasy and uncomfortable for you to do. However, it's a lot less painful than having to apologize later for erupting in a fit of flesh like a volcano that spews destructive lava all over its surroundings.

This is exactly why Jesus said, "...If thy brother trespass against thee, rebuke him; and if he repent, forgive him" (Luke 17:3). The word "trespass" means *to violate a rule; to cross a line; to commit a grievance.* Here the Bible teaches that if you believe someone has violated you, crossed a line he shouldn't have crossed, or committed what you perceive to be a grievance against you, then you need to "rebuke" that person for what he did. The word "rebuke" doesn't mean you have to speak to him like he's a devil; it means you need to directly and honestly confront him.

This issue of honesty is a big one in the Body of Christ. (I have a powerful six-tape series called "Bad Attitudes and Stinking Thinking" that deals with the subject of dishonesty in the

Church.) Many believers are dishonest about what they really think and feel. Inside they are livid with anger or ticked off with someone about a perceived offense; yet they smile and pretend like everything is all right when it isn't at all. This dishonesty secretly divides believers and keeps God's power from freely flowing between members of the Body of Christ.

According to the apostle Paul, the ability to "speak the truth in love" is one of the marks of a mature believer (Ephesians 4:15). I realize we may enjoy measuring our spirituality by how well we prophesy or speak in tongues, but that is not the mark of maturity Paul gives us. Relationships are the bottom line in life. How well we fare in our relationships with others tells the real story of how mature we are in the Lord.

Believers who have hidden disagreements or secret petty grievances against other people, yet go around smiling and acting as if everything is all right, are not just being dishonest — they're engaging in outright *lying* and *deception*.

When you refuse to be honest about your feelings and confront an offense, you are just as wrong as the one who violated your rights and stepped over the line. Until you are willing to "speak the truth in love" and be honest, you have no right to judge anyone else. You are just as wrong and you're acting just as ugly as that person is!

Remember, Jesus said, "...If thy brother trespass against thee, *rebuke him*..." (Luke 17:3). That means if you are going to be mature in your relationships, you must learn how to confront others when you feel they've wronged you. It may be hard to do, but it's a lot less painful and leaves less scars than a heart and soul filled with bitterness and resentment.

How To Confront Someone

When you have to confront someone regarding an offense that you perceive he has committed against you, I recommend that you take the following three steps:

Step #1:

Don't confront anyone until you've first made it a matter of prayer.

Prayer resolves a lot of problems by itself. There have been times in my own life when I've been upset with someone, only to discover after getting into the Presence of God and praying about the matter that my attitude was uglier than that of the one who wronged me. Once I recognized my own condition, I couldn't hold a thing against the other person anymore; I just wanted to get my own heart right before God.

Prayer will put you in a position where God can speak to your own heart. After praying, if you still sense that you are supposed to confront the other person, pray for that person first. The Spirit of God may give you a strategy regarding what to say, when to say it, and how to say it.

Believe me, taking directions from the Holy Spirit about how to confront someone will only help you. Confrontation without prayer is like barging into the middle of the fray with no preparation. Therefore, let prayer be a time of spiritual fine-tuning and preparation to do what you need to do.

As you pray, spend a few minutes thanking God for your offender. This will help bring you to a new level so you can deal with the issue at hand in the right spirit.

Remember the good things that person has done. Take time to reflect on all the good moments you've had with him and all the benefits you've gained in life as a result of that relationship. It's difficult to remain angry at someone when you are thanking God for him at the same time!

Step #2:
Don't confront anyone with a judgmental attitude.

We've all made mistakes — *and that includes you*! So assume that your offender would not deliberately hurt or offend you. Take a positive position about the other person.

When you do finally sit down to talk with the person who offended you, start the conversation by assuring him that you're sure he didn't intend to do what he did. Tell him that somehow the devil got into the middle of your relationship with him through his actions — and now you want to get the devil back *out* of the relationship as you get your heart right with him. This immediately removes any sense of an accusatory spirit and puts the spotlight on the devil instead of on that person. The issues will still be dealt with, but from a different perspective.

Starting from this approach is much more beneficial than taking a defensive approach that treats the other person as if he were your adversary. Remember, that person is not your enemy; he isn't on the other side of the line, fighting a battle against you. Your relationship may be going through some rough times right now, but you still need to view the two of you as being on the same side. The purpose of this time of confrontation is not to prove how wrong the other person is; it is to learn how to work together better and how to keep the channel of communication open and in the light.

Step #3:
Remember that you, too, have been offensive in the past.

Never forget that you've probably offended people in the past. You didn't intend to do it. You didn't even know you did it until the person later told you. You know that your intentions were not to hurt. You were probably embarrassed or sad when you heard how the devil had used some statement you innocently made to leave a wrong impression.

When you were in this type of situation, didn't you want the person you had offended to tell you the truth rather than to walk around harboring bad feelings about you? Weren't you glad when that lie of the devil was exposed and your relationship was made right again? Weren't you thankful for the opportunity to put things right with that other person?

So when someone offends you, remember that you've stood in his shoes in the past. Were you forgiven at that time? Were you shown mercy? Now it's time for you to show the same forgiveness and mercy to someone else that was shown to you in the past.

If you still feel the need to confront the person who offended you after following these three steps, you should now be able to do it with the right attitude. You have prayed about the matter; you have been in the Presence of the Lord. Now your heart is free, liberated from negative feelings and attitudes toward that person. You are finally in a position to go to that person in a spirit of love and reconciliation instead of in a spirit of accusation. As Jesus said, "...if he repent, *forgive* him" (Luke 17:3).

What Does the Word 'Forgive' Really Mean?

The word "forgive" is the Greek word *aphiemi*. It means *to set free, to let go, to release, to discharge,* or *to liberate completely*. It was used in a secular sense in New Testament times to mean *to cancel a debt* or *to release someone from an obligation of a contract, a commitment, or a promise*. Thus, it means to *forfeit any right to hold a person captive to a previous commitment or wrong he has committed.*

In essense, the word "forgive" — the Greek word *aphiemi* — is the picture of totally *freeing* and *releasing* someone. A modern paraphrase of this Greek word would simply be *"Let it go!"*

It's Time To Let It Go!

Let's look at Luke 17:3 one more time: "Take heed to yourselves: If thy brother trespass against thee, rebuke him; and if he repent, forgive him."

That means you and I don't have the privilege of holding people hostage to their past actions if they repent and ask us to forgive them. If they sincerely seek forgiveness for offending us, we are obligated to "let it go."

It is amazing how cheated our flesh feels when someone quickly repents for the hurt he has caused us. You see, our flesh enjoys holding someone's grievance over his head and making him pay for what he did — even if it's just for a little while.

But if your offender quickly repents and sincerely asks for forgiveness, Jesus said you are to *forgive* him. In other words, you must put away the offense and no longer hold on to it. You must release those ugly feelings you've held against that person. *You have to let it go!* I guarantee you, *that* is the time you find out how mature you are!

So are you able to let go of that offense? Are you able to put it away and to stop dragging it up again and again?

Exercising true forgiveness means you can no longer hold the grievance against that person. Just as God removed your sin as far as the east is from the west (Psalm 103:12), now you must decide that this person is *freed* in regard to that past offense.

Once you forgive him, you cannot drag up the offense again and again. You have released him completely; now he is freed, released, and liberated from that sin. *You never have the right or privilege to pull out that offense later and use it against him. It is GONE!*

That person is so freed from his offense against you that it can never be an issue again — at least it can't be as long as he doesn't repeat the same offense. That means you have no choice but to *let it go*!

Taking It to the Next Level

As if this wasn't already hard enough to hear, Jesus took His teaching about forgiveness to the next level in Luke 17:4, saying, "And if he trespass against thee seven times in a day, and seven times in a day turn again to thee, saying, I repent; thou shalt forgive him."

Forgiving a person who truly offended you can be a challenge. But let's say you finally work up the nerve to confront that person. You decide to forgive him and release him from the sin he committed against you. A week goes by — and then he does it *again*!

Now what are you doing to do?

Jesus said if someone trespasses against you *seven times* in one day and then turns to you seven times to sincerely ask you to *forgive* him, you are to forgive him. In other words, as long as he is willing to confess that he was wrong and is sincerely trying to change, you are to be mature enough to keep forgiving and to *let it go*! That's why the disciples answered, "Lord, increase our faith!" (v. 5).

Isn't It Time for You To Get Over It?

Forgiving someone once is one thing, but Jesus said we have to keep forgiving that person over and over again! The flesh says, "Come on, give me a break! How many times am I supposed to forgive? Does God just expect me to keep forgiving again and again and again?"

Just quit thinking those fleshly thoughts for a moment and look at the verse again! Jesus plainly taught that as long as the person tries to change — as long as he or she keeps trying to repent — you and I are to keep forgiving, even if it means we have to do it seven times in a single day!

The disciples basically said, *"Wow, Lord, if we're going to live at that high level of forgiveness, you have to increase our faith! We don't know if we have enough faith to live like that."*

Jesus' next words to the disciples were very significant. He said, "...If ye had faith as a grain of mustard seed, ye might say unto this sycamine tree, Be thou plucked up by the root, and be thou planted in the sea; and it should obey you" (v. 6). In the next chapter, I'm going to show you just how much Jesus' response reveals to us about this subject of unforgiveness.

CHAPTER EIGHT

Why Jesus Compared Unforgiveness To the Sycamine Tree

In Luke 17:6, Jesus gave an extremely vivid picture of the evil effects of unforgiveness. He also told the disciples how to get rid of unforgiveness in this verse.

Jesus said, "...If ye had faith as a grain of mustard seed, ye might say unto this sycamine tree, Be thou plucked up by the root, and be thou planted in the sea; and it should obey you." Notice that He likened the *unforgiveness* He talked about in verses 1-5 to a *sycamine tree.* Before we discuss how to uproot unforgiveness, let's first see why Jesus used the sycamine tree in this illustration. Why didn't He use a plum tree, apple tree, or orange tree? *Was there a particular reason He used the sycamine tree to symbolize unforgiveness?*

Important Facts About the Sycamine Tree

Consider these facts about the sycamine tree, and you will understand why Jesus used it as a symbol of unforgiveness. There is no doubt that Jesus chose the sycamine tree because of the following facts:

Fact #1:
In Egypt and the Middle East, the sycamine tree was the preferred wood for building caskets.

Caskets! Just think of it — the tree that was most commonly used to make caskets is the example Jesus used to depict bitterness, resentment and unforgiveness!

Why Jesus Compared Unforgiveness To the Sycamine Tree

The sycamine tree was the preferred wood for building coffins because it possessed these characteristics:

- *It grew quickly. (This was good since people needed large amounts of the wood for making coffins.)*

- *It grew in any environment (making it accessible in many different places).*

- *It grew best in dry conditions (making it easy to grow even in bad conditions).*

- *Its wood was very durable (a desired quality for the making of coffins).*

One look at this list, and I understand why Jesus likened the sycamine tree to unforgiveness. Just like the sycamine tree:

- ***Unforgiveness grows very quickly.***

It doesn't take long at all for unforgiveness to get out of control, growing so large that it starts taking over the place where it's planted — in this case, *your heart*!

- ***Unforgiveness grows in every environment.***

  It doesn't matter where a person is from, where he lives, what his culture is like, or what level of society he belongs to — unforgiveness grows in human hearts everywhere. It is *universal*.

- ***Unforgiveness grows best in dry conditions.***

  Unforgiveness flourishes where spiritually dry conditions exist. Where there is no repentance, no joy, no fruit of the Spirit — that's where unforgiveness grows and flourishes.

- ***Unforgiveness will bury you.***

  The fact that the sycamine tree was used for building caskets tells me that unforgiveness will bury you quicker than anything else! Unforgiveness is used by Satan to put you six feet under the ground. It not only works

Why Jesus Compared Unforgiveness To the Sycamine Tree

death in your physical body; it also kills your spiritual life and makes you spiritually lifeless.

FACT #2:

The sycamine tree has a very large and deep root structure.

The sycamine tree has one of the deepest root structures of all the trees in the Middle East. It is a robust tree that grows to a height of thirty feet or more.

The sycamine tree is very hard to kill because its roots go down so *deep*. Even cutting the tree down to its base doesn't guarantee its death because the roots, hidden deep under the ground, keep forcing their way to the surface to produce new life again and again.

No wonder Jesus used this tree as an example of *unforgiveness*!

Like the sycamine tree, unforgiveness must be dealt with clear down to the roots; otherwise, it will keep springing up again and again. Its roots go down deep into the human soul, and only *genuine repentance* can rip out those roots so they will stop growing back over and again.

Fact #3:
The sycamine tree produces fruit that is bitter to eat.

The sycamine tree and fig tree are very similar in appearance. The fruit these two trees produces even looks identical; however, the fruit of the sycamine tree is extremely bitter. The fruit of the sycamine looks just as delicious as a fig; but when tasted, it is very *bitter* and *unpleasant*.

Figs were expensive in New Testament times, so poorer people ate the fruit of the sycamine tree as a substitute for the fig. However, the sycamine fruit was so bitter, it couldn't be eaten whole. It had to be *nibbled* on a little bit at a time. After a pause, the eater could start nibbling again, but a person could never devour a whole piece of this fruit at one time. It was just too *tart* and *pungent* to eat at one sitting.

Why Jesus Compared Unforgiveness
To the Sycamine Tree

Like the sycamine fruit, unforgiveness is *bitter*, *tart*, and *pungent*. Most people "chew" on their feelings of bitterness and unforgiveness for a long time. They nibble on the offense for a while; then they pause to digest what they've eaten. Then they start nibbling on it again — *taking one little bite, then another and another*.

As these people think and meditate on the perceived offense, they internalize their bitter feelings toward the person or persons who offended them. In the end, the sour, bitter fruit of unforgiveness makes *them* sour and bitter as well.

Also, just as poorer people were the ones who ate the sycamine fruit, those who sit around and constantly meditate on all the wrongs committed against them are usually bound up in all kinds of poverty as well. Certainly these people become *spiritually poor* as they constantly chew on that bitter fruit. But they are also frequently *defeated, depressed, sick*, and *financially poor*.

Isn't It Time for You To Get Over It?

FACT #4:
The sycamine tree is pollinated by wasps.

The sycamine tree is pollinated when a wasp sticks its stinger right into the heart of the fruit. Since the wasp's sting initiates the pollination process, the sycamine tree and its fruit could not be reproduced without it.

This makes me think of all the times I've heard people say: *"I'm sorry, but I've been stung by that person once, and I'm not going to be stung again! What he did hurt me so badly that I'd be a fool to let him get close enough to sting me again!"*

Is it possible that these people were "stung" by a situation specially designed by the devil to pollinate their hearts and souls with unforgiveness? *Did Satan's "wasp" get to them?*

If you keep your heart free of offense, the devil cannot produce this foul fruit inside you. The best way to avoid *offense, bitterness,* and *unforgiveness* is to determine that you will *never be offended* in the first place!

Why Jesus Compared Unforgiveness To the Sycamine Tree

If you'll keep the "stinger" of that wasp out of your heart, you'll never have to uproot a huge tree of bitterness later!

It's obvious why Jesus used the sycamine tree in this illustration regarding unforgiveness.

- *Bitterness provides Satan with a perfect "coffin" in which to bury the effectiveness of your spiritual life.*

- *Its roots grow quickly and penetrate deeply to take over your mind, your emotions — indeed, every area of your life.*

- *Finally, the bitter fruit it produces is an ideal snack to "chew" on if you choose to hold on to offense and remain in spiritual and material poverty.*

But now that the problem has been identified and you better understand the seriousness of the issue, what can you do to get rid of bitterness, resentment, and unforgiveness in your life?

It's Time To *Uproot* And *Remove* That Tree!

Jesus used the illustration of the sycamine tree to tell us how to uproot and remove offenses and unforgiveness from the heart. In Luke 17:6, He gave us the secret weapon that can enable us to jerk those roots clear out of the ground and send them to a place where they will *never* reproduce in us again.

Look again at what Jesus said: "…If ye had faith as a grain of mustard seed, ye might say unto this sycamine tree, Be thou plucked up by the root, and be thou planted in the sea; and it should obey you." Notice He said, "…ye might *say* unto this sycamine tree…." In order to get rid of bitterness and unforgiveness, you have to rise up and *speak* to those destructive devices. Take authority over them with the words of your mouth!

Don't wait until you feel like doing it, because I promise you — you never will. If you depend on your feelings and emotions, you'll never be free of offense and unforgiveness.

Your feelings and emotions will tell you that you have a right and a very good reason to feel the way you do. *Therefore, you must make the choice to turn off your emotions and think with a sound mind!*

It is time for you to accept personal responsibility for this inward condition. Quit blaming everyone else for all your bad attitudes, and acknowledge that something *inside you* needs to be removed! Jesus said you must *speak* to that "sycamine tree" and tell it to *go*!

- *If you don't speak to your emotions, they will speak to you!*

- *If you don't take authority over your emotions, they will take authority over you!*

- *If you don't rise up and conquer that bitterness and unforgiveness, they will rise up and conquer you!*

Isn't It Time for You To Get Over It?

- *Quit listening to your emotions and letting them tell you what to think, what to do, and how to react.*

- *It's time for you to do the talking and take command of your thought life!*

You have to speak to *bitterness, resentment,* and *unforgiveness* like they are enemies that have come to corrupt your soul. You must make a firm decision not to tolerate this spiritual pestilence in your thought life — not even for a second. And, if necessary, you must speak to unforgiveness *again, again, again, again, again, again, and again* — until it is finally *uprooted* and *removed* forever!

You have to go for the roots! If you want to be free, it's going to take an attitude that says, *"I'm going to grab on to the roots of this beast and yank them clear out of my soul — and I'm not going to stop until I'm totally free!"*

Command Those Attitudes To Be Planted in the Sea!

Salt water won't allow a plant to grow; the salt will kill it. Therefore, once a plant or tree is thrown into seawater, it becomes a *dead issue*. It doesn't matter how hard you try to make that plant grow again, it will never happen. Its life is gone forever!

That is precisely how you have to deal with those dead issues you've spoken to and commanded to *be removed* from your life. Once you've told them to go, don't allow them to reestablish their roots again. *They are dead issues — and they are to remain dead forever!*

If your flesh calls out to you, luring you to go over all those old hurts again, *don't* allow that bitter tree to come back to life again. Throw it into the sea of forgetfulness. Bury it in the sea so deeply that its roots can *never again* regain a foothold in your soul.

Isn't It Time for You To Get Over It?

Jesus instructed us to say to the sycamine tree, "...Be thou plucked up by the root, and be thou planted in the sea...." Notice what He says next: "...and it should obey you." The word "obey" is the Greek word *hupakouo*, which means *to submit to* or *to obey*.

Your out-of-control emotions are just like an out-of-control child. They will rant, rave, and carry on all day long — *until* you finally stand up and tell them to straighten up and act right!

Flesh will pout, throw a temper tantrum, and carry on to a ridiculous extent until you decide that *enough is enough*. When you finally make the choice to rise up, speak to your emotions, and exert your authority in Jesus Christ, *your flesh will obey your commands*!

- *If you don't take authority over your emotions and flesh, they will continue to dominate and hound you.*

- *If you'll stand up to your destructive emotions and plant them in the sea forever, they will obey you, and you will be free!*

So quit allowing your flesh to be your master! It's time for you to let the Spirit of God inside you take charge and start calling the shots. Bitterness and unforgiveness have absolutely no place in your life, so *uproot* and *remove* them once and for all!

CHAPTER NINE

Ten Practical Suggestions To Keep Your Heart Free of Bitterness, Unforgiveness, and Strife

It's a fact none of us can escape. From time to time, situations arise in all our lives that entice us to get *upset, offended,* or *resentful.* These situations are usually over minor issues that get all blown out of proportion. But by the time we realize how petty the issues are, it's often too late. Bad words have already been spoken, and hurt is lodged deep in the soul. The only thing left to do is to begin the process of getting over the hurt and offense. However, this is a much more difficult thing to do than it is to just deal with the situation differently in the first place.

Because this is a predicament that everyone faces at one time or another, I've written ten suggestions that I've learned to apply in my own life to help keep my emotions in balance and my heart free of offense. These practical suggestions may not seem deep or profound. But if they help keep your heart free of strife and offense, they are *mighty* and *powerful*!

Read the following points carefully. I believe they will help you keep the door closed to the devil so he can't destroy your relationship with the people you love, the people you work with, or those with whom you serve the Lord.

SUGGESTION #1:
If you think you're getting in strife, ask to be excused for a few minutes.

I've learned that when I am weak and tired, I am more susceptible to an attack from the devil. It is amazing how many times the devil strikes our minds and emotions when we are physically or emotionally exhausted. He knows that when we're tired, it's harder to hear and see things correctly.

For instance, have you ever gotten so deeply involved in a conversation that you couldn't see your way out? I have. The longer you talk, the more trapped you feel. Even worse, you can't even remember how the tangled-up conversation got started in the first place! You're exhausted from trying to prove your point or understand the other person's view. Instead of sensing the sweet fruit of the Spirit flowing from your heart, you feel like you're about to erupt in a fit of raging carnality and say things you'll later regret.

When you find yourself in this type of situation, it's time for you to ask to be excused for a few minutes. Give yourself an opportunity to get a grip on your emotions and see things in a new light. You may be tempted to get into strife just because you are physically or mentally tired. That weariness may be affecting you so you cannot accurately hear or understand what the other person is trying to communicate to you.

Isn't It Time for You To Get Over It?

At times I become involved in a situation in which stress and strife begin to develop between me and someone I love or whose cooperation I need. If I'm tired when this happens, my perception is more easily distorted. As the conversation gets more and more intense, I sometimes feel like I'm losing track of the point we are both trying to make. Frustrations arise. Conflict erupts. I later end up regretting that I didn't put on the brakes and stop making such a big deal over something so insignificant.

That's why I've learned the wisdom of walking away from this type of situation for a short break. When I realize my emotions are getting bent out of shape about something that really shouldn't be such a big deal, I just ask for a few minutes to be by myself.

Satan loves to attack people when they are tired. So instead of letting him take advantage of you when you are weak and tired, be smart — tell the other party or parties involved in the potential conflict that you need to take a break for a little while. Go enjoy a walk around the block; take a twenty-minute nap; pray; or read your Bible. Do something that takes your mind off the issue at hand and helps you relax for just a little while before you have to come back to deal with that issue.

I'll tell you a secret I learned years ago that has helped me avoid strife in my own life. When I'm tempted to get upset with someone, I look for the opportunity to just get away, close my eyes, and sleep for fifteen minutes. When I'm able to do that, I often awaken with a brand-new approach and a positive attitude toward the problem I'm facing. Although that problem may have seemed overwhelming to me just a short time before, my little nap clears my mind and helps me get started again with a healthier outlook.

Psalm 46:10 says, "Be still, and know that I am God…." There is something about *calming* yourself and making yourself *be still* that helps you see things in a brand-new light when you return to take up a difficult conversation where you left off.

So whenever you are tempted to lose your peace and get into anger or strife, back off. Do whatever is needed to get your focus back to where it ought to be. Perhaps you need to read your Bible for a few minutes and allow it to produce peace in your soul. Maybe you need to find a private place so you can pray in tongues for ten minutes. Or you may be the kind of person who needs to do something physical to get rid of all that tension, such as jogging or walking.

Whatever you need to do to give yourself a few minutes of rest, do it. You'll not only feel better, but you'll be able to return to the situation at hand with renewed strength and a better perspective. By keeping yourself in check in this way, you'll keep your friendships a lot longer and avoid saying harsh words in moments of weariness that you'll regret later!

**Ten Practical Suggestions
To Keep Your Heart Free of Bitterness,
Unforgiveness, and Strife**

SUGGESTION #2:

If you're tempted to get upset with what someone is telling you, invite a third party into the conversation so he or she can help you hear what the other person is trying to communicate.

Sometimes when we are tempted to flare up and get into strife with someone, we are just "getting our wires crossed" and missing what that person is trying to tell us. These mishaps of misunderstanding are Satan's golden moments when he tries to wedge his way into a conversation and disrupt a relationship we cherish.

If you feel like "your feathers are getting ruffled" by something that is being said to you, it's time to use your head, tell your emotions to shut up, and invite a third party into the conversation so he or she can help you hear what is really being communicated.

I have found that the presence of an unbiased third party is often helpful. Because this person is *emotionally unattached* to what is happening, he or she can sometimes see the full picture clearer than those who are in the midst of the heated discussion.

Ephesians 4:26,27 says, "Be ye angry, and sin not: let not the sun go down upon your wrath: Neither give place to the devil." Do everything you can to stay free of anger, wrath, and strife, since these fleshly emotions give the devil free access to wage war in the situation you're facing. If bringing an unbiased person into the discussion to hear both sides helps you understand what the other person is trying to say to you, you have taken a very wise step toward disarming the devil and preventing him from doing his business!

So lay down your pride and admit you need a third opinion to help you hear more clearly. You may be surprised to find out that you were wrong and that the other person really did have something smart to contribute! A third person may be the very ears you need to help you see through the muck of misunderstanding.

Suggestion #3:

If your conflict is with someone who is in a supervisory position over your life or work, remind yourself that you are to speak to that person with respect.

If you're tempted to get upset with your boss, pastor, or someone who holds a supervisory position over you, remind yourself that the Lord has placed him in that position. You must treat that person as someone God has placed in authority over you, even if you don't like what he is saying or doing to you at the moment. Never forget that *you* are under *him*; it isn't the other way around. If you adopt any other attitude, you'll end up being *subversive* to that God-ordained authority in your life.

You may say, "Yeah, but you don't know how hard it is to work for this person!"

That may be true, but who twisted your arm and forced you to take that position? Didn't you agree to submit to this situation when you took the job? If you don't like it, there are other places to work or to serve. No one is making you stay where you are — *unless*, of course, the Lord has placed you there and told you it is where you are supposed to be.

"What if it's a work situation that developed after I took the job?" you may ask. Well, you can rest assured that it didn't take the Lord by surprise. *Is it possible God has placed you in this position to reveal something that needs to change inside you?*

If the Lord has placed you there, you need to do your job with a smile on your face. Do everything in your power to go through each day with a happy heart. That may mean you have to spend more time with God. Whatever it takes, determine that you will do it.

Otherwise, you may allow your heart to become filled with scorn toward that leader and end up in rebellion against him and his orders. In that case, you would really be rebelling against God, since He is the One who told you to take that position and work with this person in the first place!

Hebrews 13:17 says that you are to *obey* your leaders. The word "obey" is a military term that describes soldiers who know how to honor and respond to their immediate authority.

It is not the job of a soldier to correct his commanding officer. Rather, it is the soldier's responsibility to advise, help, and honor his leader by obeying his orders.

Therefore, if the person in authority over you is doing something that collides with your convictions so that you cannot follow his lead, you need to remove yourself and go somewhere else where you can work or serve with joy. Better to remove yourself from the situation than to get into strife and open a door for the devil.

Get alone with the Lord. Let the Holy Spirit speak to your heart and put the situation in right focus for you. Read, read, and *read* Titus 2:9: "Exhort servants to be obedient unto their own masters, and to please them well in all things; not answering again."

Let the divine instruction in that verse sink deep in your heart. It will help you stay free from rebellion and strife when a difference of opinion arises between you and those who are in a supervisory position over you.

Suggestion #4:
Don't allow yourself to become a judge of another person's inward motivation.

God is the only One who sees the heart. You may think another person's actions reveal a heart that isn't right with the Lord. But you really don't know what is in that person's heart, so leave it alone. *Don't get into the judgment business.*

Jesus warned us, "Judge not, that ye be not judged" (Matthew 7:1). The fastest way to get a pile of judgment dumped on you is to dish it out first!

**Ten Practical Suggestions
To Keep Your Heart Free of Bitterness,
Unforgiveness, and Strife**

When you feel yourself tempted to start judging another person's inward motivations, put on the brakes and stop it as quickly as possible! Judgment results in judgment. That means you're headed in a direction that's going to bring judgment right back on your own head!

Refuse to get involved in the judgment business. Let the Lord deal with the deeper matters of someone else's heart that you can't see nor correct. Instead of getting upset with that other person, take a look in the mirror and ask yourself if you are the one who needs to change and grow up this time.

I seriously doubt that you are always right and others are always wrong. Is a pharisaical spirit trying to operate in you — the fleshly attitude that demands to be right all the time? *No one is that perfect.*

You need some time to reassess what you're seeing, hearing, and feeling. Go to the Word of God and let its light shine into the deepest recesses of your heart so it can expose any inward attitudes that are wrong. Before you assume everyone else is wrong and you're right, see if you're the one who needs to change this time!

No one is *always* right! Everyone is wrong from time to time. No one is perfect in his opinion or his assessment of a situation. It's all right to back off and let someone else be right.

So before you start getting upset and pointing your emotional finger at others, first go take a good look at yourself. Find out if YOU are the one who is wrong in this particular situation!

Suggestion #5:
Realize that your opinion is just your opinion.

Moral absolutes are not debatable; however, most conflicts that arise are not over moral absolutes. Most conflicts are centered around issues about styles, choices, or mere differences of opinions.

**Ten Practical Suggestions
To Keep Your Heart Free of Bitterness,
Unforgiveness, and Strife**

Don't let a difference in style, choice, or opinion become bigger than it ought to be. If there are one hundred people in the room, there will probably be one hundred different styles, choices, or opinions about some subjects.

As long as these subjects are not important doctrinal or moral issues, don't get all bent out of shape. These are not the kinds of issues to get upset about or to fight and cause division over. They are just differences of style, choice, or opinion; therefore, don't be guilty of "…teaching for doctrine the commandments of men" (Mark 7:7).

You have to learn to separate major issues from minor ones. Most conflicts are centered in the minor category. So before your flesh becomes upset because others see things a little differently than you do, stop to ask yourself, *Is this really so serious? Or is this merely a difference of opinion in the minor category?* Don't make a major out of a minor.

Suggestion #6:
Learn to be flexible.

Conflicts often arise when a change occurs in one's schedule or priorities. *But change is unavoidable in life.* Every believer must develop the ability to adapt to a changing environment, for God is always telling His people, "Behold, I will do a new thing; now it shall spring forth; shall ye not know it?..." (Isaiah 43:19).

Anything that remains stagnant all the time is either dead or on the verge of dying. Tell yourself that change is not always bad. Ask the Holy Spirit to help you make the adjustments needed to "go with the flow."

Sometimes change is good for us because it forces us into a new or higher mode of thinking. We must learn to accept change as God's way of taking us to a higher level in our attitude and performance.

One thing is certain: Inflexibility leads to stress and conflict. If you are a part of an organization or a church that is experiencing growth, you'll find that it has to regularly reorganize and restructure to accommodate that growth. If you are someone who demands that everything stay the way it is right now, you'll find yourself constantly feeling upset and frustrated. It won't be too long before you are left behind in the dust.

You see, that growing organization or church will keep on growing whether you like it or not. Sadly, if you're resistant to change, the very thing you're resisting will soon outgrow you.

Now, change just for the sake of change isn't wise because it causes instability. But change with purpose — with a justified reason that leads to a higher and better end result — is worth doing some bending and flexing in order to bring it to pass!

Take a look at every major corporation that has touched the world, and you'll see that each one regularly updates itself so it can remain viable in today's market. Any corporation that refuses to do this will be overtaken by its competitors and will lose the edge it once held.

For instance, I remember back when the electric typewriter first came on the scene. It was a marvel of technology to the world's typing population. Then later computers were introduced to the general public. That really made waves in the business world!

To adapt to the new computer technology, people had to learn how to let go of the past to embrace the present. Imagine what the world would be like today if the business community had refused to leave their electric typewriters behind! For the world to be interconnected as it is today, it was essential for people to embrace a *change*.

If you can't handle the changes that go along with growth, it would be better for you to go join another organization or church that is satisfied with the status quo. Maybe it just isn't in your heart to be a leader; therefore, you'd rather stick with the old ways of doing things.

But if you choose to move forward and take a progressive approach to life, you must ask the Holy Spirit to help you make the adjustments needed to "go with the flow." You also must believe that God is truly able to direct those who are in authority over you.

If the situation you are in has revealed inflexibility in your character, it has already been a good experience for you. It has shown you where you need to develop and mature so you can achieve what God has called you to do. Rather than feeling threatened, you can choose to see that God is working to change you. If you take this approach — if you choose to look for and find the hand of God in the situation — it will remove any threat you may feel.

SUGGESTION #7:
Give others the benefit of the doubt.

People often act in a way that is misperceived by others. Maybe they don't realize how their actions are being perceived and therefore project attitudes or actions that are contrary to what they actually intended.

Have you ever been misunderstood? Has anyone ever called your motives into question? Did it shock you to hear what others perceived about you, especially when you knew your intentions were right?

This happens to everyone from time to time. Just as you want others to believe the best about you, it's now time for you to reverse that grace and believe the best about others. Jesus gave us this principle in Luke 6:31 when He said, "…As ye would that men should do to you, do ye also to them likewise."

So when an offense occurs, assume that the person didn't intend to be offensive. Give the same grace to others that you want others to extend to you. Give them the benefit of the doubt. Mercy is never wrong.

**Ten Practical Suggestions
To Keep Your Heart Free of Bitterness,
Unforgiveness, and Strife**

SUGGESTION #8:
Be forgiving when others act ugly.

When someone rubs you the wrong way and you're tempted to get offended or upset because of that person's flaws, remember how often God has had patience with your *own* flaws and faults.

Before you become too condemning, put the situation in the right perspective. Ask yourself, *Have I ever acted ugly or spoken an unkind word?* Chances are that you've done the very same thing to others that this person you're upset with has done to you!

Speak to your emotions when you are tempted to get offended or to get into strife. Remind yourself to accept others just as Jesus Christ has freely and graciously accepted you.

Romans 15:7 says, "Wherefore, receive ye one another, as Christ also received us to the glory of God." How did Jesus receive you and me? Did He require perfection of us first, or did He take us just as we were at the time we came to Him?

Isn't It Time for You To Get Over It?

Praise God, He took us just as we were, with all our attitude problems, defects, inconsistencies, and blemishes!

Since you've been saved, have you ever done anything to disappoint the Lord? Have you ever allowed yourself to act in a manner that was unbecoming for a Christian? Have you ever entertained ugly thoughts or accusations about someone else? Yes, of course you have. Yet Jesus has never cast you away or become so disgusted that He's disowned you.

According to Romans 15:7, we are to receive each other just as Christ has received us. That means we need to do a lot of forgiving and overlooking in life!

I strongly advise you to quit concentrating so fiercely on the faults and flaws of others, and start concentrating on how to be more forgiving and merciful. *If you give mercy, you'll be shown mercy.*

**Ten Practical Suggestions
To Keep Your Heart Free of Bitterness,
Unforgiveness, and Strife**

Take the route of mercy, and you'll never be sorry! Believe it or not, there are times when you're supposed to shut your eyes to what you saw that other person do and just let it go!

If you'll take this approach to life, you'll have a lot less emotional disappointments and problems with your nerves. Just give people the same forgiveness and mercy you want others to extend to you.

SUGGESTION #9:

Ask yourself: *Would I want someone else to respond to me in the same way I am responding right now?*

When my flesh wants to rant and rave about an injustice it thinks has been done to it, I am tempted to be very bold and aggressive with my offenders. This is usually the time when unkind words are spoken or extreme statements are made that get all blown out of proportion.

When I am tempted to get upset, I ask myself, *If this situation were turned around and someone was upset with ME, would I want that person to react to me with this attitude?* Of course, the answer is *no*!

In Philippians 2:3, Paul tells us, "Let nothing be done through strife or vainglory; but in lowliness of mind let each esteem other better than themselves." When dealing with another person, always go the route of preferring and esteeming that person better than yourself. As you do, you'll rarely speak an unkind word or allow your flesh to rant and rave.

Ask yourself, *Do my attitudes and actions reflect the esteem and honor I would like to receive from others if the situation was reversed and I was the object of rebuke?*

SUGGESTION #10:
What would Jesus do in this situation? What instruction has the Holy Spirit given you?

Jesus went to the Cross and died for those who hung Him! He could have called twelve

Ten Practical Suggestions
To Keep Your Heart Free of Bitterness,
Unforgiveness, and Strife

legions of angels to come to His defense; instead, "...he threatened not; but committed himself to him that judgeth righteously" (1 Peter 2:23).

Is it possible that you need to keep your mouth shut and follow in the steps of Jesus this time (1 Peter 2:21)?

Most often it is better to go the way of the Cross and allow God to be your Defender. Of course, you must deal with problems when they arise, especially if they are of a severe nature. But never forget that God is a God of justice. Let Him be the Defender of your dreams and ideas.

The Holy Spirit may show you other ways to shut the door to resentment, offense, bitterness, and strife. If you will listen to Him, He will show you how to circumvent the attacks the enemy tries to wage in your soul against your family, friends, and fellow workers.

If you refuse to listen to the Holy Spirit, you can expect grudges, resentments, hostilities, animosities, and anger to begin building up inside you with every unresolved conflict and added offense. In the end, your bitter, angry attitudes will separate you from the people you normally get along with and dearly love.

When Satan's "hook" is firmly set, those lies and wrong emotions will become a stronghold in your life. You'll begin to rationalize and find logical justifications for holding on to those killer attitudes — *even though you know they are wrong.*

Don't let Satan sink his hook in you through offense! Follow in the footsteps of Jesus, and go the way of the Cross. It may seem painfully difficult at the moment, but I guarantee you that it isn't as painful as a heart full of bitterness, resentment, and strife!

So What Are You Going To Do?

Once you've made the choice to grab hold of God's grace and let Him take you over these emotional hurdles, don't ever let the devil drag you

Ten Practical Suggestions To Keep Your Heart Free of Bitterness, Unforgiveness, and Strife

back into the bondage of bitterness and offense again. *Stay free!* It's time to rise up and take charge of the situation in *your* soul. Remember, it is your soul, and you are responsible for what happens there.

The Holy Spirit is present *right now* to help you make the choice to forgive and forget. You can permanently walk free of what others have done to you — or what you *think* they did to you.

It doesn't matter who was right or wrong in the situation. What matters is that you uproot the tree of bitterness before it begins producing deadly fruit in your life. If other believers really did commit an offense against you, God will deal with them. After all, they are His children too.

So ask the Holy Spirit today to come alongside you and help you turn from those feelings of bitterness and unforgiveness. Then expect Him to empower you so you can speak with authority to the bitterness that has kept you bound for too long. Tell that bitterness to GO in Jesus' Name — and then walk free from offense once and for all!

Greek and English New Testament Study Helps

Reference Book List

1. *How To Use New Testament Greek Study Aids* by Walter Jerry Clark (Loizeaux Brothers).

2. *Strong's Exhaustive Concordance of the Bible* by James H. Strong.

3. *The Interlinear Greek-English New Testament* by George Ricker Berry (Baker Book House).

4. *The Englishman's Greek Concordance of the New Testament* by George Wigram (Hendrickson).

5. *New Thayer's Greek-English Lexicon of the New Testament* by Joseph Thayer (Hendrickson).

6. *The Expanded Vine's Expository Dictionary of New Testament Words* by W. E. Vine (Bethany).

7. *New International Dictionary of New Testament Theology* (DNTT); Colin Brown, editor (Zondervan).

8. *Theological Dictionary of the New Testament* (TDNT) by Geoffrey Bromiley; Gephard Kittle, editor (Eerdmans Publishing Co.).

9. *The New Analytical Greek Lexicon;* Wesley Perschbacher, editor (Hendrickson).

10. *The Linguistic Key to the Greek New Testament* by Fritz Rienecker and Cleon Rogers (Zondervan).

11. *Word Studies in the Greek New Testament* by Kenneth Wuest, 4 Volumes (Eerdmans).

12. *New Testament Words* by William Barclay (Westminster Press).

Books by Rick Renner

BOOKS IN ENGLISH

Seducing Spirits and Doctrines of Demons
Living in the Combat Zone
Merchandising the Anointing
Dressed To Kill
Spiritual Weapons To Defeat the Enemy
Dream Thieves
The Point of No Return
The Dynamic Duo
If You Were God, Would You Choose You?
Who Is Ready for a Spiritual Promotion?
It's Time for You To Fulfill Your Secret Dreams
Isn't It Time for You To Get Over It?

BOOKS IN RUSSIAN

How To Test Spiritual Manifestations
Living in the Combat Zone
Merchandising the Anointing
Dressed To Kill
Spiritual Weapons To Defeat the Enemy
Dream Thieves
The Point of No Return
The Dynamic Duo
Hell Is a Real Place
What the Bible Says About Water Baptism
What the Bible Says About Tithes and Offerings
Signs of the Second Coming of Jesus Christ
Who Is Ready for a Spiritual Promotion?

BOOKS IN GERMAN
- Dream Thieves
- The Point of No Return
- Dressed To Kill
- The Dynamic Duo

Tape Series by Rick Renner

Ministry and Servanthood (16 tapes)
The Anointing (4 tapes)
Miracles of Jesus Christ (8 tapes)
The Person, Power, and Work
    Of the Holy Spirit (12 tapes)
Aggressive Worship (3 tapes)
Spiritual Warfare Vol. 1 & Vol. 2 (6 tapes each)
Abraham, Father of Faith (10 tapes)
Samuel, Spokesman of Almighty God (10 tapes)
Prayers of the Apostle Paul (12 tapes)
Seven Messages to the Seven Churches
    In the Book of Revelation (10 tapes)
Supernatural Direction and Guidance (10 tapes)
Six Important Messages to Leaders Today
    (6 tapes)
Taking a Stand…in Difficult Situations (6 tapes)
Getting Rid of the Past (6 tapes)
How To Respond If You've Received the
    Judas Kiss (6 tapes)
Overthrowing Strongholds (6 tapes)
Keys to Winning the Race of Faith (6 tapes)
Healing the Mind and the Emotions
    Of the Oppressed (3 tapes)
Fulfilling God's Divine Destiny for Your Life
    (3 tapes)
Seducing Spirits and Doctrines of Demons
    (3 tapes)
Pulling Down Strongholds (4 tapes)

- Accomplishing Your Dreams Step-by-Step (3 tapes)
- How To Survive Difficult Situations (3 tapes)
- The Holy Spirit and You (3 tapes)
- How To Improve Your Relationship With Your Spouse, Part 1 (6 tapes)
- How To Improve Your Relationship With Your Spouse, Part 2 (6 tapes)
- How To Protect You and Your Family In the Last Days (12 tapes)
- If You're in a Trap, Here's How To Get Out (6 tapes)
- The Greatest Miracles of Jesus Christ (6 tapes)
- Wilt Thou Be Made Whole (2 tapes)
- The Will of God, Key to Success (10 tapes)
- Crossing the Bridge of Fear and Torment (2 tapes)
- It's Time To Get Over Your Bad Attitudes And Fix Your Stinking Thinking (6 tapes)
- The Person and Power of the Holy Spirit (6 tapes)

Videotapes by Rick Renner

The Communion of the Holy Spirit
The Supernatural Assistance of the Holy Spirit
For We Wrestle Not Against Flesh and Blood
Biblical Approach to Spiritual Warfare
Wilt Thou Be Made Whole
Spiritual Error in the Church, Part 1
Spiritual Error in the Church, Part 2
Spiritual Error in the Church, Part 3
Qualifications of Leadership, Part 1
Qualifications of Leadership, Part 2
Submission and Authority, Part 1
Submission and Authority, Part 2
Pulling Down Mental Strongholds, Part 1
Pulling Down Mental Strongholds, Part 2
Seven Messages to the Seven Churches
 — Overview of Seven Churches
Seven Messages to the Seven Churches
 — Rev. 2, John
Seven Messages to the Seven Churches
 — Ephesus
Seven Messages to the Seven Churches
 — Ephesus and Smyrna
Seven Messages to the Seven Churches
 — Pergamus
The Help of the Holy Spirit, Part 1
The Help of the Holy Spirit, Part 2
The Help of the Holy Spirit, Part 3
Right Foundations, Part 1

Right Foundations, Part 2
New Supply of the Spirit
The Power of the Tithe
How To Survive in Difficult Situations, Part 1
How To Survive in Difficult Situations, Part 2
Abusive Situations in Work and Marriage, Part 1
Abusive Situations in Work and Marriage, Part 2
Abusive Situations in Work and Marriage, Part 3
Proper Attitude for Pursuing Your Purpose, Part 1
Proper Attitude for Pursuing Your Purpose, Part 2
How To Make Every Minute Count

For Further Information

For all book orders, please contact:

Teach All Nations

A book company anointed to take God's Word to you and to the nations of the world.

A Division of
Rick Renner Ministries
P. O. Box 8540
Tulsa, OK 74101-8540
Phone: 1-877-281-8644
Fax: 1-888-281-4868

*For prayer requests
or for further information about this ministry,
please write or call
the Rick Renner Ministries office
nearest you (see following page).*

ALL USA CORRESPONDENCE:
Rick Renner Ministries
P. O. Box 1709
Tulsa, OK 74101-1709
(918) 496-3213
Or 1-800-RICK-593
E-mail: renner@renner.org
Website: www.renner.org

RIGA OFFICE:
Rick Renner Ministries
Unijas 99
Riga LV-1084
Latvia
(371) 780-2150

MOSCOW OFFICE:
Rick Renner Ministries
P. O. Box 14
Moscow 109316
Russia
7 (095) 298-1174

KIEV OFFICE:
Rick Renner Ministries
P. O. Box 205
Kiev 01025
Ukraine
380 (44) 248-7254

OXFORD OFFICE:
Rick Renner Ministries
Box 7, 266 Banbury Road
Oxford OX2 7DL
England
44 (1865) 308387
E-mail:europe@renner.org

NOTE:
To order a complete audio, video, and book catalog, please write to our offices in Tulsa or Oxford.

About the Author

Rick Renner is a highly respected leader and teacher within the global Body of Christ. Rick ministered widely throughout the United States for many years before answering God's call in 1991 to move his family to the former Soviet Union and plunge into the heart of its newly emerging Church.

Following an apostolic call on his life, Rick works alongside his wife Denise to see the Gospel preached, leadership trained, and the Church established throughout the world. Today Rick's broadcast "***Good News with Rick Renner***" is seen in nearly one hundred nations. He has distributed hundreds of thousands of teaching audio and videotapes, and his best-selling books have been translated into the four major languages in use today. Rick is also the founder of the Good News Association of Churches and Ministers, through which he oversees and strengthens hundreds of churches in the territory of the former Soviet Union.

Rick Renner Ministries has offices in Belgium, England, Latvia, Russia, Ukraine, and the United States. Rick, Denise, and their three sons have homes in Riga, Latvia, and Moscow, Russia.